A Desperate Faith

Other books by Jo Kadlecek

Nonfiction

Woman Overboard: How Passion Saved My Life

Desperate Women of the Bible: Lessons on Passion from the Gospels

Fear: A Spiritual Navigation

Reckless Faith: Living Passionately as Imperfect Christians

Feast of Life: Spiritual Food for Balanced Living

Fiction

A Mile from Sunday, book 1 in the Lightfoot Trilogy

A Quarter after Tuesday, book 2 in the Lightfoot Trilogy

A Minute before Friday, book 3 in the Lightfoot Trilogy

The Sound of My Voice

a Desperate Faith

LESSONS OF HOPE
FROM THE RESURRECTION

JO KADLECEK

BakerBooks
a division of Baker Publishing Group
Grand Rapids, Michigan

© 2010 by Jo Kadlecek

Published by Baker Books
a division of Baker Publishing Group
P.O. Box 6287, Grand Rapids, MI 49516-6287

Printed in the United States of America

ISBN 978-1-61664-635-6

Published in association with the literary agency of Alive Communications, Inc., 7680 Goddard Street, Suite 200, Colorado Springs, CO 80920. www.alivecommunications.com.

They had expected a walkover, and they beheld a victory; they had expected an earthly Messiah, and they beheld the Soul of Eternity.

Dorothy L. Sayers, "The Triumph of Easter,"
Letters to a Diminished Church

God raised him from the dead, and for many days he was seen by those who had traveled with him from Galilee to Jerusalem. They are now his witnesses to our people.

Paul, in Acts 13:30–31

Contents

Introduction

IMPOSSIBLE STORIES

Last fall, I planted bulbs in the front of our house. Daffodils, lilies, tulips, crocuses, you name it. I went a little crazy because it felt like a junior high science experiment and I wondered if it'd work. If it did, I knew that by spring I'd be seeing petals.

For urban types like me, gardening experience is limited to a few window boxes from community block parties. So I consider it downright amazing to bury one thing in the ground and have it emerge months later something altogether different. It seems an impossible feat: in spite of concrete, asphalt, or broken beer bottles, flowers with colors as bright as any New York taxi can burst forth.

Granted, this "new" concept is anything but. Yet, when I remember holding the hard, colorless round bulb in my hand only to see "it" now bulging with a green stem and yellow petals, I can't help asking, How did that happen? Forget science class—this is a magic show.

Of course, we don't *need* flowers in front of our homes or apartments to survive each day. Give us a roof over our heads, a cup of water, and a piece of bread. We'll make it. Like more people in the world than we want to admit, you and I really can exist in simple conditions.

Even so, I'm convinced every human does indeed *need* the magic of nature, of art and color and story, to move beyond existing and enter that place where we live fully, or at least, well. We *do* need words that spring forth from flower beds, that speak of newness and beauty and hope all wrapped up in one. If nothing else, we need the colors and fragrances of a changing season like spring to soften the concrete struggles around us. They keep us going. They inspire.

That's the nature of resurrection.

To be sure, this undercurrent of the Christian life, this subtext of every story we encounter—death, resurrection, transformation—runs deep in our collective soul. It is the theme of more songs and films, paintings and novels, missions and centers than any other in the history of art (which is the history of humanity). We cheer for the underdog on the screen who conquers each obstacle set in her path; we marvel at the painting that stirs some feeling we'd forgotten we had. We turn the dial, change the channel, or visit another creative ministry until we connect to a song or an image that draws us to a new place, a new perspective, a new way to press on.

We're wired to hope. To look forward, not backward. To find beauty and goodness and truth in spite of the gloomy contrast within and around us. We crave it intuitively, looking always for the stuff that helps it emerge within us like lilies in the spring. We want to believe the impossible. Why? My guess is we know there is more to this earthy existence.

Thank God there is.

After Jesus died, he went for walks on the beach. *After* he spent three days buried in the soil of death, he cooked breakfast for a few friends. He chatted and lingered on sidewalks and in gardens, telling stories, holding hands, eating bread. Sure, he lived well *before* he died. Admirably. Heroically. Boldly. But *after* he died—that is, *after* his lungs collapsed and his heart stopped—he spent the next month and a half strolling through the Middle East; forty full days of handing back hope to women who'd lost it, reminding men of the truth of Scripture, encouraging hundreds of friends that there was indeed more to this world than what they saw each day as the sun came up.

Yes, that was some living.

And those days on earth after his execution were apparently so full, so exciting and rich, that John says he couldn't record them all in his Gospel account (John 20:30–31). Maybe the Risen Christ drew pictures in the sand; maybe he sang hymns with his friends. Maybe he picked figs or went fishing or danced jigs. Whatever else he did in his resurrected life—apart from the stories we do have—history testifies to the reality that he gave us plenty to keep reveling in the wonders of living.

To keep planting bulbs and watching for petals.

That is what this book is about.

It is, you could say, a collection of impossible stories, of flowers that miraculously change. There are the stories, of course, from the Gospel narratives from which we might discover new truths about a Living Messiah perhaps we'd never seen before, hoping to find some new beauty we might have missed for all their familiarity.

But you should know, too, that there are other stories in the chapters which follow, parables really that I hope will help cast a new light on the ancient ones. Many are drawn from recent history. But they are equally true stories and equally reflective of the magic—or miracle—of what happens in the garden of a human heart when the Person of God in Jesus appears. Perhaps such testimonies will serve as a sort of lens through which your perspective of the Gospel narratives is sharpened. Or perhaps it will be the other way around.

Either way, the characters and conflicts, deaths and lives that emerge in the many stories—both biblical and modern—that follow reveal both a history and a future. My hope is that as you read them, you will see the seeds of the living Word emerge, familiar and yet unknown, despairing and yet hopeful, sad and yet overflowing with joy. Because *after* Jesus died, he spent what I call "very-much-alive-time" with utterly desperate friends, so much time—enough time, that is—that the stories of *their* lives changed history. His death planted in them new life.

And what happened to them also happened to others, and others beyond them. It still does. Miracle stories indeed. Impossible new beginnings. Spring fragrances.

Bright daffodils that once were only hard dull bulbs. A desperate faith that blossoms into hope all because a Holy Presence dug through the soil to make a garden.

Finally, Pilate handed him over to them to be crucified.

John 19:16

1

Desperate Truth

We really can't avoid it. We will get to the good news, I promise. But first we have to start at what many would call the end of the story. The execution. The funeral. The place and heartache of death.

It was a moment in history like many others: a seemingly innocent man was falsely accused, condemned in a mock trial, and sentenced to death for his radical claims and dangerous acts. He was tortured, whipped, and thrust naked upon a cross with stakes piercing his arms and feet, then left to suffer one of the most excruciating and inhumane forms of death penalty the world has ever known. Hundreds watched. Many ridiculed him.

The long, painful death wreaked havoc on his organs, his muscles, and his joints, adding unimaginable distress on his wrists and feet. The sky darkened and the agony accelerated. Eventually, his lungs couldn't hold up from the pressure and he took his final breath. His organs failed. His heart stopped. And when there was no life left in him—just to add a final misery—some thug grabbed a spear and pierced his ribs. Finally, the bloody and bruised corpse was removed from the tree and left in a tomb for later burial.

Jesus was dead.

I think of many leaders across the centuries who experienced similar treatment—being falsely accused and sentenced to die for statements they made or movements they led. I think of early Christians fed to the lions for sport, European Protestants or Catholics burned at the stake by monarchists, indigenous people slaughtered on every continent, abolitionists attacked in England and America, Jews gassed by Nazis, missionaries threatened in jungles, civil rights workers shot in America's southern states. The list is endless because an endless number of men and women have stepped forward in some of the ugliest and most perilous times in history to fight an injustice and instead lost their lives in gruesome executions. In place of respect, death became the penalty for what they believed. And many across today's globe still risk all they have for what they consider to be true.

It is not a happy ending for any story, as noble or honorable as it might be: death for a hero means he will never again see his family or friends on this earth. His leadership has ended.

But this was not just any death, because this was not just *any* man. Those who'd known him knew this to be true.

And so, for those who came to Golgotha to watch the execution of the carpenter from Nazareth, the man they'd come to love, the despair must have been horrendous. The women and men who'd spent three intimate years listening to the young rabbi must have battled cruel emotions after his murder. No doubt they became disillusioned, grief-stricken, and desperate in profound and terrifying ways. What truth would they cling to now that their Messiah had been publicly killed? What hope did they have for a better life? Why hadn't he saved himself if he really was who he said he was?

How could it happen? Why would it? What now?
God *was* dead.

The Broken Precedent

What they didn't realize—indeed could *not* realize—was that
this man's death was hardly the end of the story. It certainly
looked that way because by human terms it *had* to be that
way. Death was final. Everyone knew that when a person's
human heart stopped beating, he was lost. He would no
longer talk or think or love. He was gone for good. Forever.
His soul might live on somewhere, and his memory would,
of course, stay with those he left behind. But dead meant a
life was over. Period.

And this young man from Galilee was certainly dead.
They'd seen him murdered with their own eyes. A few had
even stood close enough to watch as the corpse was dropped
from the tree and carried to a grave. The next day their grief
and fear must have paralyzed them. And the next day as well.
Until a few of them—women, to be specific—managed to
pull themselves together enough to make their way to the
lifeless body and prepare it for proper burial.

But on that early morning road, they got a hint that this
man's story had not, in fact, ended at all. If anything, it
was now—in a most confounding and unexplainable way
at that—beginning, really beginning. Not just as a page in
another chapter either, but as an entirely new book. A new
world. A new hope. A new life.

The essence of the Christian faith throughout history, after
all, is rooted not merely in what happened when the Lord died,
in the beautiful sacrifice he made for the sins of humanity.
But the heart of Christianity has been the literal heartbeat
of what happened *after* death.

It was *after* his lungs collapsed and his heart stopped that
something truly bizarre occurred: the once-dead man became
alive again and actually walked around the Middle East for

forty days—as God, yes, but in flesh-and-blood human form as well. He visited with friends in a garden, chatted with them on the road and in their apartments, even cooked breakfast for them on the beach.

But make no mistake: it was this group of completely disenchanted men and women, those who'd watched him die and who were now feeling more discouraged and directionless and desperate than they ever had in all their lives, that he appeared to. This ragtag group of scruffy fishermen and former prostitutes, who'd been unreliable, hot-headed, and wishy-washy even when they'd traveled with him and were now all the more vulnerable because their leader had been killed—*these* were the folks he appeared to.

They were dead in hope. He was alive in the flesh. Their lungs were filled with despair; his were brimming again with oxygen. They were terrified and despondent and alone; he was hungry and singing and present.

Why? Why did Jesus, the God-man, spend forty days on the dusty roads of earth *after* his death, when he could have returned home to the majesty of heaven? After all he'd suffered during his execution, the pain and loneliness and shame, how in the world did he come back to life? Why would he want to? How did he beat death, and why did he stick around for not just a couple hours but several weeks? And out of all the powerful and elite people on the planet at that time who could have helped him get a major movement off the ground, why did he seek out these bumbling scaredy-cats, these women and men from the margins of the world?

At the cross, they must have plummeted into despair, enormously disillusioned, having watched their leader accosted and dragged away by the power brokers of the day. Who wouldn't? Most of us know what it's like to invest all of our trust into someone we're convinced will make our lives and the world better—a candidate, a pastor, a friend—only to be devastated when a crisis reveals that it is not true. When the boss fails, the friend betrays, or the senator lies, we're crushed. Despondent. Hopeless.

But there he is. Breaking the precedent of death and appearing just when they—when we—were convinced it couldn't get much worse. To make good on his promise. To remind them that he was right all along. To encourage them to keep going. To tap them on their shoulders and point to an ending when everything really will be happy.

That story is only going to get better and better with each turn of the page—with Jesus, the Risen One, the Word made flesh who dwells among us as the only man in human history who died and lived again and does not stop living.

The Believable Proof

The stories of the resurrected Christ interacting with his followers—recorded in the Gospels of Matthew, Mark, Luke, and John as well as in the book of Acts—are the point and purpose of this book. Early on in my Christian journey, I skimmed them. At times I studied them with a highlighter and an occasional thick reference book. But mostly I'd kept them at a distance, inspired by their snapshots of Jesus but unsure what difference these resurrection stories made in my daily life of faith. In some ways they became like those other harder-to-believe stories of the Bible. Give me Paul's letters, Christ's sermons, or David's psalms—these words had direct application to my life. But Jonah in the belly of the whale? Jesus alive *after* he had died? What was I supposed to *do* with those? I knew they mattered to a life of faith; I just didn't know *how*.

Then a few years ago I got word that my mother was sick. She was being taken to a hospice, and within days I was sitting beside her as she lay on a sterile white bed. I held her hand. My family gathered around her. Shortly after, I watched her struggle for her last breath. And then she was gone. It was a profoundly terrible experience. And not long

19

after, my stepmother also got sick, and the same process was repeated.

The gravity and intimacy of death stunned me so that I began looking anew for some way to make sense of the despair I felt over losing these women. I was daunted by regret. I was troubled by lost moments. I knew there was *hope in Jesus*, but that was beginning to feel like a pat answer: cold but probably right, though not directly helpful during this time.

I'd learned long ago, though, to reach for a Bible anyway, regardless of how I felt or didn't feel. Maybe it was because of the stark intersection between death and life that I began to turn again to the stories of Christ's resurrection. I began to wonder how his friends must have felt. I listened to his words to them as I stayed in the last pages of each Gospel for weeks, reading them over and over. I got out pens and notes and many more thick books, and I began to talk about them with my husband. We rambled on and on about each story, we talked them over with friends, and I even taught about them at retreats.

I came to realize that I had rushed over the reality of Christ's resurrection and rushed even faster over the stories of his interactions with his followers. Yes, I'd acknowledge them each Easter season and paid lip service to the Resurrection as the most important aspect of our shared faith. I'd say I believed, at least intellectually, that the resurrection is true and actual, but—and maybe you can relate to this—I hadn't yet come to view it as a source of wisdom or perspective for today like, say, Proverbs or Colossians; a nice moment in Christian history, maybe, inspiring for *then* but somehow not getting through to contemporary minds *now*.

Yet the resurrection radically changed those early followers of Jesus. Yes, the risen Jesus had affected every single aspect of their lives—from their finances and jobs to their relationships and families. Mine, however, seemed anemic in comparison.

There are many possible reasons for this. Though history has testified of the millions who across cultures and continents have believed this resurrection story since the days of the early church, I, as a product of the twenty-first-century Western world, too often view it as merely an afterthought for modern life, a tiny memory in my faith that flickers against the massive engines of global progress. As my life gets busier, I tend to get more "self-sufficient." Maybe you can relate. My work days grow longer while my relationships and beliefs become fragmented. I'm bombarded regularly with media on every side of every day and often confuse real life with the virtual one of the Internet. I have fantastic entertainment on demand but often forget the greatest story of all.

Maybe that's the problem. Maybe I've come to view Christ's resurrection in the same way we would a really good action, adventure, and romance movie all rolled into one. It's got a compelling story line, great special effects, characters we care about, and even (especially important for Americans) a happy ending. When I "watch" it, I get a nice feeling that lingers for a few days, until another compelling story grabs my attention.

Granted, if we attend a local Christian church, we might hear about the resurrection of Jesus a little more, but not much. Christians, too, tend to treat it like we do our favorite flick, and at least once a year—say, every Easter—remember, "Gee, that's a great story." We pop it in the DVD player to watch it one more time before cleaning the house or going to work. We're warm and fuzzy from its familiarity but rarely changed by it. We don't always know what to *do* with it.

It's also possible that we've sentimentalized the risen Lord during a season of chocolate and bunnies because we don't know quite how to believe in an empty tomb. It is no small thing, especially in a frantic culture saturated with constant noise, to stop long enough and consider something so . . . impossible. Yes, we're hungry for a truth that trumps all the hype of our culture, but how could the resurrection be better than the latest iPod or Oscar-winning film? We long for a lasting relationship, but how can the Word made flesh compete with all our emails, text messages, and Internet communities?

Who has time to slow down and come face-to-face with something so ancient and intangible as resurrection?

Yet considering the state of our high-tech cultural chaos, as well as the personal despair we'll inevitably face at the loss of a loved one, maybe the better question is, who of us can afford *not* to?

To be honest, that question has gnawed at me since I attended my mother's funeral. Because if the stories around Christ's resurrection *are* true, wouldn't they be as relevant to us today as every other book of the Bible? What might we be missing each time we race through those stories that surrounded the central aspect of the Christian faith? And as my husband and I have asked each other during these last few years, what would our lives look like, *really look like*, if we actually believed that Jesus spent forty days with his friends *after* he died?

Would we confront death any differently if we were confident of the resurrection? How would we live in this decaying world if the resurrection really was the center of our being?

These questions are also the point of this book.

After all, the stories of Christ's interactions with his followers after his death provide some of the most incredible narratives of any sacred writing within any religion. Each chapter fills out a little more of the picture of the ministry and work of the Risen One. Each reveals a unique aspect of his mission and character as we read how he imparted both to individual disciples as well as to the community of believers. But as stories within a larger narrative, they also can be a little tricky to follow in their entirety.

That said, it might be helpful to think of the Gospel accounts of Christ's resurrection in the same way we might think of letters we'd receive if four friends took a trip to the Holy Land for several weeks and then each decided to write home. They would probably mention many of the same sites they visited, but they would also include varying details because their perspectives and their audiences would be unique to their situation. All four would be *true* accounts of their trip, only each would emphasize elements they found important to their reporting.

In the same way, the Gospels highlight different aspects of the same incredible event; they complement each other. And yet they retain their own unique styles. Matthew, for instance, reveals a Jewish sensibility as well as details that he, as a tax collector and young Jewish professional, would have noticed. His account, probably the second Gospel written, addresses Christ in terms of his kingdom for a Jewish audience. Though Mark is the second of the Gospels in the New Testament, most scholars believe his was the first written. Mark's audience was Greek, and he structured his narrative based on words from Peter, who was an eyewitness to most of Christ's ministry.

Luke, another young professional but not Jewish, was a doctor and very much aware of the social issues and implications of his day. Consequently, his record is based on many interviews and careful research (see Luke 1:1–3) and features more stories of women and other marginalized people than the other Gospel accounts. And John's Gospel, the last written, emphasizes the character of Christ so that those reading or hearing it might believe and grow in their salvation.

I think of these four writers this way: Matthew and John were confidants in Christ's inner circle; Luke and Mark were followers of those influenced by Matthew and John and were also really good journalists. All were inspired by God to write about the Lord's time on earth sometime during the first century after his crucifixion.

In other words, these four Gospel accounts of Christ's life, death, and resurrection offer various elements of the same astonishing story, nuanced anecdotes for understanding a much, much bigger picture. The more I study them, the more I find (and keep finding!) how consistently rich with detail and historic observation they are; they take us to an unparalleled time on earth, to an event that literally altered the human story. And yet, as one author wrote almost a hundred years ago, "The evidence for the resurrection is not so much what we read in the Gospels as what we find in the rest of the New Testament—the new life of the disciples. They are a new group. When it came to the cross, his cross, they ran away. A few weeks later we find them rejoicing to be beaten, imprisoned and put to death (Acts). What had happened?"[1]

When Jesus encountered his utterly desperate friends *after* his death, as well as another five-hundred-plus people (Paul tells us), something changed for them. Whether the women at the tomb, the disciples in the upper room, or the fishermen on the beach, their hearts were no longer despairing when this Man stood before them. They were delighted! They'd watched every terrifying part of his execution and now with those same eyes were watching his arms and legs move again, not as some superpower angelic vision or apparition, or even some cool special effect in a movie, but in physical form. As a man who was now walking beside them. They heard his voice. They smelled the fish he cooked over the fire. A few touched his ankles, one even poked his ribs.

This dead man they'd loved was alive? That *would* change everything. And from that point forward, Christ's resurrection became the reason for their life together. It defined church history, so much so that many faith-filled martyrs were burned at the stake or sentenced to death because of it. They regarded these encounters with the Son of God as true stories, actual events that defined the center of their beings, the primary purpose for living at all. They grounded their lives on the reality of Jesus Christ's resurrection from a gruesome death and were willing to believe both events actually happened, no matter what it cost them. It was no intellectual exercise or weekly confession for them.

For Jesus, of course, it was all very normal. He was simply continuing his mission. During his forty days of resurrection, he continued to console his grieving friends, as he had throughout his three-year ministry. He continued to confirm the truth of his words as he had with each sermon or healing across Jerusalem, and he continued to commission his followers with the news of eternal life in him.

He hadn't changed. During his post-death time on earth, he was merely doing what he'd always done: pursuing those he loved. But for them—for Peter and Mary, John and Thomas, and the others who'd seen his battered body and were now watching the same shaggy-haired man eat and hearing him laugh and talk—how could they *not* be transformed? It was a moment of complete upheaval in all they'd ever called reality; their lives were radically altered the moment they *knew* that Jesus was alive. He redefined *real* for them.

"Because I live, you also shall live," he'd said.

So it wasn't a movie? Not some fairy tale or fantastic Greek myth or cool interactive website?

No. It is instead the point on history's time line around which the rest revolves, a fact as *factual* as the fall of the Roman Empire or the creation of Michelangelo's *David* or the signing of the Declaration of Independence. To be sure, the triumph of his living presence has been at the heart of more social changes, more political agendas, more movements for good than any other single influence on any continent in any time period. More stained glass windows have been dedicated to this single story; more mosaic walls, painted ceilings, sculpted stone, and grand symphonies have been created around this history than all the creative efforts of other religions combined. As J. R. R. Tolkien said, "There is no tale ever told that men would rather find true, and none which so many skeptical men have accepted as true on its own merits. . . . This story is supreme; and it is true. Art has been verified."[2]

Jesus is alive. And if he is indeed, how can our lives be the same?

His followers knew the answer. They, in all their grief and cowardice and lack of faith, were transformed by his presence; we can be as well. Their stories are far more than a morsel of wisdom for the day; they are an invitation to participate in the impossible, to feast on the Bread of Life today and tomorrow and forever so that, as with the early church, those around us will never be the same.

Exploring the Claim

British theologian N. T. Wright wrote (in one of those thick books I found):

> The truly extraordinary thing is that this belief was held by a tiny group who, for the first two or three generations at least, could hardly have mounted a riot in a village, let alone a revolution in an empire. And yet they persisted against all the odds, attracting the unwelcome notice of the authorities because of the power of the message and the worldview and lifestyle it generated and sustained. And whenever we go back to the key texts for evidence of why they persisted in such an improbable and dangerous belief they answer: it is because Jesus of Nazareth was raised from the dead. And this provokes us to ask once more: why did they make this claim?[3]

We started this chapter with the death of Jesus. In the same way the text was evidence of his execution, the stories we are about to read and explore are evidence as well of his life and interaction with his followers. They give us clues to the "improbable and dangerous belief" that allowed them to persist against all odds, igniting a movement that has been nothing short of revolutionary. Each story—like each letter from our four friends visiting the Holy Land—offers unique details and perspectives for understanding Christ's purpose on earth and in the kingdom to come. They are tools in the hands of the Creator as he shapes our lives around the most astonishing fact that's emerged out of any culture.

But we will need help in studying them if they are really to seep into our souls and usher in change. Each will require our imagination and faith as well as our desperation to come like the disciples in their grief: raw, anguished, in need of an impossible triumph.

As we do, each story then opens a door that introduces us to another side of the Risen One.

The Resurrected Christ talked with many individuals but also crowds; he fished and ate, walked and laughed, and as a result, his friends, family, and hundreds of believers' lives were utterly transformed. The question for us will be the same as we travel through each account: How, too, can we be changed? How does the resurrection matter in our daily lives? How do these narratives of the Risen Jesus instruct us?

The story began with one man's death two thousand years ago. It changed a few at first. And then a few more. And countless since. It was a death perhaps like few others, but what happened after inspired more change, more acts of mercy and kindness and grace than the world had ever known, deeds that continue even now. For in those forty days, a few desperate women and men got the shock—and the hope—of their lives. Nothing was ever the same again for them.

May it be the same of us.

—— IN-BETWEEN REFLECTION ——

1. Stories shape our thinking and teach us about living. What books or stories from your childhood particularly affected your view of hope? Of death? Of love? How?

2. Describe the first time you remember hearing about the crucifixion of Jesus Christ. What made it significant to you?
3. Can you recall a memorable Easter? What happened?
4. How do you think people today respond to the resurrection of Jesus Christ? Do they generally consider it important in their daily lives? Why or why not? What does it mean for you today?
5. Why do you think Jesus walked the earth for forty days after he died? Was there something significant about that number?

PRAYER:

May your death, dear Jesus, stir in me a deep sense of gratitude and humility as I look anew and with wonder at the reality of your life on earth. Amen.

PREPARATION

Please take a few moments right now to read Matthew 28:1–15 and Luke 24:1–12, both printed below. It is the first account recorded in Scripture of Christ's empty tomb, which several women discover. Once you've read it, pause for a quiet moment to consider the words you've read.

MATTHEW 28:1–15

After the Sabbath, at dawn on the first day of the week, Mary Magdalene and the other Mary went to look at the tomb.

There was a violent earthquake, for an angel of the Lord came down from heaven and, going to the tomb, rolled back the stone and sat on it. His appearance was like lightning, and his clothes were white as snow. The guards were so afraid of him that they shook and became like dead men.

28

The angel said to the women, "Do not be afraid, for I know that you are looking for Jesus, who was crucified. He is not here; he has risen, just as he said. Come and see the place where he lay. Then go quickly and tell his disciples: 'He has risen from the dead and is going ahead of you into Galilee. There you will see him.' Now I have told you."

So the women hurried away from the tomb, afraid yet filled with joy, and ran to tell his disciples. Suddenly Jesus met them. "Greetings," he said. They came to him, clasped his feet and worshiped him. Then Jesus said to them, "Do not be afraid. Go and tell my brothers to go to Galilee; there they will see me."

While the women were on their way, some of the guards went into the city and reported to the chief priests everything that had happened. When the chief priests had met with the elders and devised a plan, they gave the soldiers a large sum of money, telling them, "You are to say, 'His disciples came during the night and stole him away while we were asleep.' If this report gets to the governor, we will satisfy him and keep you out of trouble." So the soldiers took the money and did as they were instructed. And this story has been widely circulated among the Jews to this very day.

Luke 24:1–12

On the first day of the week, very early in the morning, the women took the spices they had prepared and went to the tomb. They found the stone rolled away from the tomb, but when they entered, they did not find the body of the Lord Jesus. While they were wondering about this, suddenly two men in clothes that gleamed like lightning stood beside them. In their fright the women bowed down with their faces to the ground, but the men said to them, "Why do you look for the living among the dead? He is not here; he has risen! Remember how he told you, while he was still with you in Galilee: 'The Son of Man must be delivered into the hands of sinful men, be crucified and on the third day be raised again.' " Then they remembered his words.

When they came back from the tomb, they told all these things to the Eleven and to all the others. It was Mary Magdalene, Joanna, Mary the mother of James, and the others with them who told this to the apostles. But they did not believe the women, because their words seemed to them like nonsense. Peter, however, got up and ran to the tomb. Bending over, he saw the strips of linen lying by themselves, and he went away, wondering to himself what had happened.

When you are ready, continue reflecting on the following question:

Perhaps you've read this story before. What new insights or observations did you notice as you read the story anew in these two Gospel accounts? Jot them down. Take a few moments to reflect before reading the next chapter.

PRAYER:

Dear Lord, help me to hear the truth in the midst of distractions and deceptions so that I may reflect it to others, for your sake. Amen.

2

Unlikely Witnesses

During the last few months of 1999, our country, indeed the world, was gripped by the reality of a daunting moment in history: a new millennium. The term *Y2K* (Year 2000) was dropping from nearly everyone's mouth, provoked by the expectation of pandemonium when computer clocks switched from 99 to 00. The concern was warranted; computer scientists in the 1960s had apparently not anticipated the importance of *four* digits, so that when the computerized systems rolled over to the year 2000, they would interpret 00 as 1900. In other words, the difference between January 1, 2000, and December 31, 1999, would be calculated as one hundred years rather than one day!

The Y2K glitch affected not only computer software but also the hardware, and consequently, it threatened to disrupt every major industry around the globe, from utilities and banking to manufacturing and airlines and everything else with computer files. People feared Y2K would wipe out accounts, cut off insurance policies, or shut down utilities.

Countless books were written, television shows aired, and "survival kits" mass marketed to a worried public. Grocery stores sold out of bottled water, flashlights, and canned goods, and media speculation only fed the paranoia. Around every corner and across every newspaper, the same mantra of doom echoed: we were going down. When the ball dropped in Times Square on New Year's Eve 1999, the world as we'd known it would end. Or at least come very close.

My husband and I had traveled to Sydney, Australia, that Christmas, on our way to visit his parents just north of Brisbane. Even in the land down under, people were desperately afraid, a sign that countries everywhere were bracing for the inevitable chaos and probable destruction that the year 2000 would bring.

But something else was happening in Sydney at that time as well. I saw it with my own eyes as we walked one late afternoon from the beautiful Sydney Opera House and around Circular Quay, Sydney's hub for a busy harbor. I still remember looking across the water as passenger ferries, fishing boats, and cruise ships passed by. The sun was just setting, and I marveled when I saw a series of lights switched on across the Sydney Harbour Bridge. As each lit up, it was as if someone's huge hand was writing out one single word: *Eternity*.

Eternity. From anywhere in the harbor, there was no mistaking the letters that had been shaped and hung across the world's largest steel arch bridge in Australia's largest city. Nearly 160,000 vehicles crossed the bridge each day that year, connecting commuters and tourists to the many surrounding suburbs and beaches. The bridge, which today is an international symbol of Australia, was the centerpiece of the city. And at the end of 1999, city officials had decided to display this solitary word across their most prominent feature.

Of course, the lighted *Eternity* was a part of the city's New Year's Eve festivities, and it was lit up every night at dusk several weeks prior to the last midnight of 1999. But why *Eternity*? Why not *Happy New Year*? Or *Good luck* or, given the Y2K tone of fear and destruction, *Condolences*? When the entire world would be watching Sydney's New Year's Eve televised events first since their time zone meant they'd see 2000 before anyone else in the world, why did Aussie organizers pick the word *Eternity* to highlight the center of their festivities?

My husband, who once lived in the city, told me the answer: from the early 1930s into the mid 1960s, people walking throughout Sydney would often come across a strange little piece of "graffiti" on the sidewalks. Written in white or yellow chalk and in perfect copperplate script on paths and streets across the city was the word *Eternity*. At first officials assumed the chalk message was the work of a few thugs. But because it never appeared on anything but public footpaths and was always written in the same perfect copperplate script, they eventually deduced that only one person was responsible for the writings.

For years no one actually saw the messenger scribbling the word on the sidewalks, but around every corner *Eternity* greeted them. Whether hurrying to work or on their way home, people literally would step on the word, glancing quickly at it as they moved on their way. Speculation and fascination fueled the urban legend, and many locals claimed responsibility because of the public attention they would receive. But inevitably the deceivers were proved wrong, and the author remained a mystery.

Finally, some twenty-five years after the first *Eternity* appeared on the sidewalk, the reverend of a small Baptist church wandered in to his parish early one morning. He saw a slight, gray-haired man, no taller than five foot three, bending over, chalk in hand, and recognized him as his church janitor.

"Why, Arthur," said the minister, "are *you* Mr. Eternity?"

Startled that he'd been caught, Arthur looked up at his pastor and answered, "Guilty, your honor."

The local newspaper found out and sent a reporter to the minister, who identified the author of *Eternity*. The puzzle had been solved, though Arthur Stace kept writing his word, probably over half a million times, and trying hard to avoid getting caught. He'd rise early in the morning, before the city crowds would come, so as not to be seen; he would pray and then go where he believed God had directed him, writing the word every hundred yards or so on the pavement. He saw his mission as evangelistic but never wanted any publicity. In fact, he feared it.

Then in 1967—two years before Arthur would die at the age of eighty-three—another reporter tracked him down and learned more of his story: he'd grown up in cruel poverty, landed in jail as a teenager, and been shipped off to France as a soldier during World War I. He returned to Sydney an alcoholic, partially blind, and without a job. He was desperate, hungry, and especially hopeless. So when he heard a Baptist church was serving meals, he went.

There Arthur heard a preacher talk about eternity. Arthur recalled to the reporter that when he left the church, that single word—*eternity*—kept ringing in his brain. He broke down and sobbed. And from that point, his life changed radically. He said he felt a

> a powerful call from the Lord to write "Eternity." I had a piece of chalk in my pocket, and I bent down right there and wrote it. I've been writing it at least 50 times a day ever since, and that's 30 years ago. The funny thing is that before I wrote it I could hardly write my own name. I had no schooling and I couldn't have spelled "Eternity" for a hundred quid. But it came out smoothly, in a beautiful copperplate script. I couldn't understand it, and I still can't. I've tried and tried, but "Eternity" is the only word that comes out in copperplate. I think Eternity gets the message across, makes people stop and think.[1]

It certainly did make people stop and think—so much so that his word, and his story, stayed in the minds of local Aussies; a statue was erected in Arthur's honor, a documentary film was made on his life, numerous poems were written about his "chalk" ministry, and the National Museum of Australia in Canberra even named one of its galleries the *Eternity* gallery, chronicling Arthur's life and chalk ministry.

It was an obvious choice, then, for Ignatius Jones, the key producer of Sydney's 1999 New Year's Eve celebration, to honor his legacy. Jones was impressed that Arthur had come back from the war so despairing and yet somehow able to "reinvent" himself by bringing joy and meaning into people's lives. Not only did the word symbolize the mystery and magic of the city, but Jones called it the ideal word for the New Year's Eve: "On this night of fellowship and good cheer, it shouldn't just be about one night. The word says that this celebration should be eternal in human life."[2]

And so in the midst of the desperately fearful Y2K moment in modern history, God's reminder of unending life burst surprisingly across a beautiful bridge to usher in a new millennium. All because of an unlikely messenger whose life had been changed by a single encounter many years before.

Encountering the Word

My husband took a photograph that night we saw *Eternity* light up the Sydney Harbour Bridge. It hangs now on our living room wall and reminds me daily not only of a wonderful trip but also of the faithful witness of a broken man whose love for Jesus had literally been written across the city where he lived. I believe his influence continues every time someone looks at that photo in our living room or visits the Eternity gallery in Canberra, because his story reveals how a desperately hungry alcoholic discovered something he never thought possible—hope—and then could not stop telling others the same.

But he was not exactly bold in his telling. It took twenty-five years for his identity to be revealed. In fact, I imagine that every time he bent over to write his *Eternity* "sermon," he experienced a mix of emotions, much like the joy and trembling that the first witnesses might have felt at Christ's empty tomb. Matthew recorded it in verse 8 of chapter 28: "So the women hurried away from the tomb, *afraid yet filled with joy*, and ran to tell his disciples" (emphasis added). Like them, Arthur was exuberant in the reality he'd encountered, a reality that had changed his life. Still, he was fearful of how others might treat him if they caught him scribbling. No matter how he might have tried, though, he could not keep the news to himself, even if that meant planning as cautiously as possible to stay out of the public's eye. Who, after all, in downtown Sydney—the center of the country's commerce—*wanted* to be confronted daily with the news of eternity?

And who of the desperate men and women who'd followed a young rabbi, now slain, *wanted* to be confronted with the ridiculous news these first witnesses conveyed? They were already terrified at what might await them *without* their leader; they were guilty by association, and if local authorities had murdered Jesus, what violence might await his followers? Were their lives in danger because of their devotion to the dead Jesus? Probably. Was their community now threatened with the possibility of disintegration? Absolutely. So they'd kept out of the public eye, congregating secretly in apartments or fields, hoping no one would catch them as they grieved their enormous loss. And as they tried to determine what on earth they would do next, they likely would have had little patience for the absurd fairy tale they were about to hear from these women.

Yes, the last thing they expected was a message of hope. And they certainly did not expect to hear it from the most unlikely witnesses in Jerusalem, those who'd ventured early in the morning to the tomb. No wonder the women were *afraid yet filled with joy*: they'd encountered the reality of the resurrection in the face of disturbingly chaotic times. Both were cause for terror.

And yet something enormously joyful compelled them, like Arthur, to tell the others, despite what might await them.

The Context of the Tomb

Before we explore this first encounter with the risen Jesus, establishing some guidelines for studying these passages from Matthew and Luke as well as the stories that follow might be helpful. I've used these same guidelines in my own personal study, in retreats where I've been privileged to teach, and in my book *Desperate Women of the Bible: Lessons on Passion from the Gospels*, which explores the stories of the nameless women in the Gospels who encounter Jesus. Because many reading friends have told me they've also found these guidelines helpful in navigating specific passages, I hope they will serve us here as we look at these stories.

The first question we'll ask is what is the *context* of the passage? What's happened in the culture and to the characters in the story that might affect its meaning and its message? What's the bigger picture in which this scene is set? The context question helps us better understand all of Scripture as a unified book and keeps us from creating theologies (or belief systems) that might spring up from an isolated verse. Compartmentalizing verses—or taking them *out* of context— is always dangerous. We must not forget that God's Word is one sacred text, comprised of many layers and nuances that blend together to reflect God's deeper purposes.

Next we will ask what *conflict* exists in the passage. Conflict not only drives every piece of literature (nonfiction and fiction alike) but also reveals the tensions within the characters that might be derived from external circumstances. As we understand such tensions, we'll also understand the needs that will be addressed—needs, I suspect, much like our own. So let's consider: Who or what is being confronted? Who or what forces are at odds? In other words, what aspect in the story needs to be redeemed, what bad needs a touch of good, what evil chaos needs to be tamed and ordered by righteousness? Is there someone lost who needs saving or redirecting?

When we understand the context of each story and what the conflict reveals about the people and the culture in which they live, we can begin to ask what *counsel* this story has for us. What can we learn about Jesus within the details and the dialogue of the story? What new insights could we gain? What does the story teach us? For undoubtedly each life, each interaction, each passage has a purpose and probably a lesson. Our job, with the help of the Holy Spirit, is to discover at least a portion of its wisdom and glean from its truth at the moment we encounter it.

But lest each step become merely an academic exercise, we must finally ask the most important question of all: who experiences conversion in the story, and how can their change—like Arthur's—lead *us* on our spiritual journey for the sake of others? How can it help *us* change, and how can we then be agents of such change to those around us? Who experiences genuine *conversion* because of their encounter with Christ, and how can we?

Each step—context, conflict, counsel, and conversion—assists us in the regular conversation we have with God through Scripture. And as these questions guide us through this passage in Matthew 28:1–15 (and those that follow), my hope is that they'll deepen our understanding of and love for the hope of the ages, the Son of Man, Jesus Christ. In each passage we'll see a little more of how he comforts his people, confirms his Word to them, and commissions them for greater works than they could ever imagine.

I think it's safe to say that none of this would have been on the minds of those Jewish women who first visited Christ's tomb on that now famous Sunday morning. No, in fact, grief was a dark cloud over them. Passover week had ended in agony for them, and now after two long and painful days, they crawled out of bed long before the sun came up and desperately hurried to the tomb. They carried their spices in anticipation of the gruesome but ceremonial task they assumed awaited them once they arrived. They were to prepare the corpse of their beloved young rabbi for proper burial. And from every indication, that was the only thing they expected to do.

But why so early in the morning? Why not go mid-morning or later that afternoon? Perhaps, like Arthur Stace, they believed this would be the "safest" time for them to complete the duty they'd been given to fulfill. Maybe they wanted to avoid being seen or avoid certain people (men) altogether. Or maybe the ground was cool and the body not yet reeking from the stench of death and decay.

Each reason is probable given the cultural context. But what matters more is simply this: all the Gospel writers confirm that women were the first to visit the empty tomb on the third day. And each writer reports that they'd come early in the morning three days after Christ's death, thereby having bestowed on them the extraordinary identity of *first* witnesses of an empty tomb.

Who were these women? In chapter 23, verse 55, Luke identifies them as those "who had come with Jesus from Galilee." They "followed Joseph [of Arimathea] and saw the tomb and how his body was laid in it." Once they received their mission from the angel, Luke specifically identifies them (in 24:10): "It was Mary Magdalene, Joanna, Mary the mother of James, and the others with them who told this to the apostles."

So Mary Magdalene, Joanna, Mary the mother of James, and the others (and we don't know how many others were there) were at the grave where the dead body had been laid and were the first to relay the message that there was no dead body! Were they mad? Were they delusional? No. In fact, back in chapter 8, verses 1–3, Luke gives us a bit of their back stories:

> After this, Jesus traveled about from one town and village to another, proclaiming the good news of the kingdom of God. The Twelve were with him, and also some women who had been cured of evil spirits and diseases: Mary (called

Magdalene) from whom seven demons had come out; Joanna the wife of Cuza, the manager of Herod's household; Susanna; and many others. These women were helping to support them out of their own means.

First, Mary, whose life had been plagued with demons until she met Jesus, was the same Mary who had an intimate conversation with the risen Jesus, recorded for us in John 20, which we'll look at more in the next chapter. Joanna was married to a prominent authority figure in the king's court, yet somehow she had the freedom to travel with Jesus while her husband continued his work. She was clearly a woman of means who was so drawn to Jesus that she willingly devoted herself to him and to caring for the company of his ragtag followers. That meant she sacrificed her own comfort for him as well as for formerly troubled women like Mary.

Because no husband is mentioned, Susanna was likely a widow or single. Her ministry was simply to Jesus, and like the others, she ministered to him and his following out of her own means and time. There is also the other Mary, Matthew tells us, who commentators have concluded was probably the wife of Clopas (who walked with his companion on the Emmaus road) and sister of the mother of Jesus. In other words, this Mary was one of Christ's aunts.

The fact that these women had been traveling with Jesus and supporting him from their own expense accounts is unparalleled in ancient history. To have had women in this patriarchal society not only devoted to a religious leader but also traveling *with* him would have surely appeared scandalous. In this culture, women were second-class citizens and therefore relegated to the fringes of society. They were considered inferior, irrelevant, and unteachable, even to the point that most rabbis refused to offer spiritual lessons to them and legal authorities gave them no credibility in a court of law. In fact, women were not allowed to offer testimony during any trial exactly because their word was considered meaningless.

So it is no small thing that *all* the Gospel writers place these women first at the tomb.

But why were women the first witnesses, there in a dark cemetery, of the most astounding event any culture or religion ever experienced? Isn't their mere presence both highly problematic and thoroughly inconvenient, given the male-dominated culture in which they lived? If the early church had wanted to start a revolution, wouldn't they have chosen Peter or James or anyone *but* women to investigate and tell the news of their *missing* rabbi? Or if the Gospel accounts of the resurrection were works of fiction, any literary critic would deem them unbelievable for exactly this reason. Who would believe a *woman* with such significant news? Why put the most important message of the plot, the major turning point of the story, in the hands of very minor characters?

Because it was *not* fiction.

Raining with Tension

Let us establish then that the Gospel writers reported women as the first in the cemetery simply because that was what happened. Surely the last thing anyone expected was what they found—or rather did not find—at the cemetery. Though some Jews believed resurrection would eventually occur, most in their culture looked askance at the idea. Theirs was a culture that viewed death in much the way we do today—inevitable, regrettable, real, but not quite understandable. In other words, no one expected Jesus to be anywhere but where a corpse was supposed to be.

As N. T. Wright put it, "Everybody knew that dead people did not return, that Resurrection in the flesh appeared a startling, distasteful idea, at odds with everything that passed for wisdom among the educated . . . and yet . . . Christianity was born into a world where its central claim was known to be false. Outside Judaism, no one believed in resurrection and to pagans, fame was the only real immortality."[3]

So here were these faithful women followers, utterly despairing, wretchedly grieving, arriving at the tomb with no expectation of anything but death. Next they were confronted with armed guards as well. What would they do now? How would they get inside to prepare the body? What a conflict of emotions they must have experienced as they looked from the bulking muscles of these guards to their baskets of spices.

But before they had time to think much or create a plan, they experienced not just a light morning sprinkle but a violent earthquake. The massive boulder at the entrance of the tomb moved, revealing *nothing* inside. The guards froze like dead men. The women trembled. And out of nowhere, not one but two grand angels suddenly appeared, dazzling and glorious and big. They took a seat on top of the rock, and these Jewish women, unlike their male counterparts in biblical literature who would have fallen prostrate at such a visitation, stood there shaking. Luke says they bowed their faces. Surely as Jewish women they would have known of their sacred history and expected inevitable disaster. They were mere mortals, after all, and no one could endure the presence of a supernatural being like this one, let alone two! When the women finally caught their breath, they also caught a glimpse of what stood before them and shook.

But the angels' words were gentle and knowing, and Mary and Joanna and the others did a remarkable thing: they listened. "Do not be afraid, for I know that you are looking for Jesus, who was crucified. He is not here; he has risen, just as he said. Come and see the place where he lay. Then go quickly and tell his disciples: 'He has risen from the dead and is going ahead of you into Galilee. There you will see him.' Now I have told you" (Matt. 28:5–7).

Or as Luke described it: " 'Why do you look for the living among the dead? He is not here; he has risen! Remember how he told you, while he was still with you in Galilee: "The Son of Man must be delivered into the hands of sinful men, be crucified and on the third day be raised again."' Then they remembered his words" (24:5–8).

As if the stakes weren't already high—their Messiah had died, tough guards guarded the tomb, and an earthquake had just blasted open the grave, shaking the ground beneath them and plopping massive heavenly creatures above them—now they were being entrusted with the message that the man they had come to bury was not here? He was *alive*? *Go*, the angel said to the shaking, trembling, wide-eyed, second-class females. *Go and give those cowardly brothers of yours this preposterous message—that someone who was dead is not dead any longer!*

Right.

No wonder they ran—a good quick pace—afraid and yet filled with joy. So many emotions and agonizing feelings must have been zipping through them like pinballs: execution, guards, earthquake, angels, messages—it was all so . . . confusing. Such intensity in so few days. What on earth would the disciples think now when these women appeared, sweaty, hysterical, and wild?

I suspect if they'd not been scared out of their wits they might have thought better of showing up where the disciples were hiding. Or at least they would have cooked up some explanation about the empty grave. Instead, they just ran.

Until Jesus appeared. Suddenly. He met them with a simple "Greetings" (Matt. 28:9). There they confronted the walking dead-alive man, touched his feet, and worshiped him. They recognized his authority. They heard his voice. They experienced his compassion.

They knew that what the angels had said was true: Jesus—whom they'd watched die—was somehow alive and standing in front of them!

The Counsel in the Garden

These astounding first glimpses of the resurrected Son of God with heartbroken women in a garden offer us much for the

43

times in which we live. First, the women approached the tomb as disillusioned, marginalized, second-class citizens; they left fearful yet exuberant messengers with a purpose. They thought they were going to fulfill an age-old burial ritual and instead were shocked to receive a brand-new mission. They confronted the reality of God's presence and were startled by the comfort he offered for their despair, yet immediately they were sent to tell others—to scribble on the sidewalk—that it was as he said it would be. They encountered both angelic beings and a living Jesus, and in the process an entirely new reality.

But as they ran, so too did the opposition; the guards somehow woke up from their paralysis and sprinted to the chief priests with the weird news of an empty grave. The elders called a meeting, rubbed their chins, and concocted a scheme at the same time as they helped themselves to the congregational funds. They paid the guards to spread a lie, and the guards took the money, probably to the local pub where they rambled on about how Jesus's body was stolen, instigating a skepticism about his life that's continued to this day.

In other words, the women's journey, like so many Christian journeys, was paved with a smattering of emotions and potential antagonism, yet they listened to what seemed both impossible and possible at the same time. They took their Lord at his word, and they obeyed, as can we, no matter what others might say and no matter how we might feel.

Still, there's the question of the garden: why did Christ's first appearance happen in a garden and not somewhere else? Say, a mountaintop or the middle of a river or at least in a temple? Why not make a spectacular entrance back into the land of the living, somewhere where there'd be a crowd of important people, like where the chief priests had gathered in the synagogue? Why not at least exploit the moment in a public relations stunt that would attract every man, woman, and child in Jerusalem? A mountaintop would do that, surely, or a stroll across the surface of a busy river. Wouldn't these have been better, more effective locations to show off this impossible feat, to blast across the public square the message that the executed young rabbi was alive again?

But Jesus Christ did not choose a busy intersection with masses of people. And he didn't make a fantastic entry back into the center of society when he rose from the dead. Instead, he chose a cemetery, a tomb in the middle of a garden at a time when no one was likely to be there except a few lonely mourners. Woeful souls. Desperate and despondent. Not a crowded place but a quiet, solemn one. Not a popular temple or hurried road but near a depressing, empty, smelly tomb.

The garden, in other words, forces us to look straight at the face of death, to see burial linens in a grave so that we remember just how concrete and real Christ's death was. It is an opportunity to remember each funeral we've ever attended and reimagine it as shockingly vacant. The garden symbolizes for us, as it has for the church through the ages, a place of growth and grace. Instead of appearing in a locked room, the dead-alive Christ appeared first in a garden, connecting us to the roots of our spiritual heritage where God first met Adam and Eve, even when they invited sin and death into the human race.

This garden, though, where Mary and Joanna and the others came early in the morning, held the Second Adam, Jesus, who invites us into new life, covered in forgiveness of sins because of the blood he spilled on the cross. His death provides us an opportunity to make right what happened in Eden, and his empty tomb is the only way that's possible at all, empowering us with the privilege and call to be messengers and stewards throughout the earth.

The apostle Paul described it this way in his letter to the Ephesians: "his incomparably great power for us who believe. That power is like the working of his mighty strength, which he exerted in Christ when he raised him from the dead"

(1:19–20). So the same power that raised Christ from the dead enabled the women to run with the news, and that power remains available for those of us commissioned with his purpose of eternity.

Change in the Air

When the angel told them to go, the women turned to run. They were willing to burst into the presence of their friends to tell them what the angel had said: Christ had risen. But all they'd seen at that point was a big rock moved to reveal a vacant tomb. Nonetheless, having only seen grave clothes folded inside that tomb, they took off with the news, ready to barge in on a bunch of scruffy, desperate fishermen. Who knows how the disciples would have responded to their report? Would they have thought the women insane? Would they have interrogated them for details about how they knew he was alive if they had not *seen* him with their eyes? Maybe someone *had* stolen the body. Or maybe they would have interpreted the news this way: Jesus—who was dead—was now in the other world. He had already risen into heaven.

He had not risen here. Not now. Could any of them have expected to see him face-to-face, including these women?

Yet they'd left the angel and were on their way to tell their friends about the empty grave when Jesus stopped them. Why? So they could see him with their own eyes? So they could be sure themselves of what in fact they were about to do, what news they were about to convey?

Absolutely!

Once they encountered the dead-alive Jesus with their own eyes, touched his feet, and heard his words, they were changed for good. Their world was no longer dark with terror; it was alive with the light of hope! They didn't just have a message to share with their friends; they had a person to introduce to them. Alive from the dead. Victorious over decay. Eternal over mortality.

He was the Person of Eternity, now appearing to them in the flesh. That made all the difference for Mary, Joanna, Susanna, and the others. He was not an idea or a theology or even a new moral order but a person with moving bones and skin that touched and a voice that rang gently in their ears. Because he was a new person before them—dead but now alive—they could be too.

I have often wondered why Jesus did not appear at a time when technology could help broadcast his message to millions throughout the world in seconds. With the Internet connecting thousands of people in towns or offices or locked apartments around the world in a matter of moments, why wouldn't he have used such a tool to advance his movement, to communicate his truths, and to reveal his plan? Or even a word on a sidewalk.

Because Jesus Christ is not a message. He is a person. Alive. And he is God. Both of course mean he cannot be reduced to an email or a website or a sound bite.

So instead, this resurrected Jesus visited a handful of desperate women two thousand years ago at a garden where corpses decayed. Why? To show them his eternal reality and then send them off with a new identity and purpose. He did the same with his disciples, who in turn told the early church, who then told others throughout the world until the news eventually reached a far-off land called Australia. There, many, many years later, a hopeless drunk sitting in a church was given a new chance and a new mission because he met a God-man who was alive. And that made a difference for eternity.

IN-BETWEEN REFLECTION

1. How does Arthur Stace's story of Eternity make you feel? Have you heard similar stories of such unique or far-reaching ministries?

2. Review Luke 23:50–53. What do you learn about Joseph of Arimathea? What kind of man was he, and why do you think the details of his life might be significant in the story about Jesus?

3. Why do you think Matthew's graveyard scene includes guards and an angel whereas Luke's describes two angels? Does it matter?

4. Can you recall a time when God asked you to go and do something and you found yourself "afraid yet filled with joy"?

5. What might be the one word that would capture your own life's purpose, like Stace's Eternity?

PRAYER:

May your eternal presence, dear Jesus, empower me anew as I serve others with your love and life. Amen.

PREPARATION

Please take a few moments right now to read from John 20:1–18, printed below. It is another account recorded in Scripture of Christ's empty tomb, which a woman discovered. Once you've read it, pause for a quiet moment to consider the words you've read.

JOHN 20:1–18

Early on the first day of the week, while it was still dark, Mary Magdalene went to the tomb and saw that the stone had been removed from the entrance. So she came running to Simon Peter and the other disciple, the one Jesus loved, and said, "They have taken the Lord out of the tomb, and we don't know where they have put him!"

So Peter and the other disciple started for the tomb. Both were running, but the other disciple outran Peter and reached the tomb first. He bent over and looked in at the strips of linen lying there but did not go in. Then Simon Peter, who was behind him, arrived and went into the tomb. He saw the strips of linen lying there, as well as the burial cloth that had been around Jesus' head. The cloth was folded up by itself, separate from the linen. Finally the other disciple, who had reached the tomb first, also went inside. He saw and believed. (They still did not understand from Scripture that Jesus had to rise from the dead.)

Then the disciples went back to their homes, but Mary stood outside the tomb crying. As she wept, she bent over to look into the tomb and saw two angels in white, seated where Jesus' body had been, one at the head and the other at the foot.

They asked her, "Woman, why are you crying?"

"They have taken my Lord away," she said, "and I don't know where they have put him." At this, she turned around and saw Jesus standing there, but she did not realize that it was Jesus.

"Woman," he said, "why are you crying? Who is it you are looking for?"

Thinking he was the gardener, she said, "Sir, if you have carried him away, tell me where you have put him, and I will get him."

Jesus said to her, "Mary."

She turned toward him and cried out in Aramaic, "Rabboni!" (which means Teacher).

Jesus said, "Do not hold on to me, for I have not yet returned to the Father. Go instead to my brothers and tell them, 'I am returning to my Father and your Father, to my God and your God.'"

Mary Magdalene went to the disciples with the news: "I have seen the Lord!" And she told them that he had said these things to her.

When you are ready, continue reflecting on the following question:

Perhaps you've read this story before. What new insights or observations did you notice as you read the story in John's Gospel account? Jot them down. Take a few moments to reflect before reading the next chapter.

PRAYER:

Dear God, thank you for calling me by name. May I have ears to hear your voice and eyes to see your presence, for your glory. Amen.

3

Name's Sake

Isabella was born with the wrong color of skin. In fact, most of her young life in the early 1800s in New York was wrong: she was a female, black as night, and gangly as a newborn calf. All were strikes against her that only made worse the identity she was born into: slave.

Because her owner, Johannis Hardenbergh, was a Dutch-speaking farmer, Isabella's first language was Dutch. Shortly after Hardenbergh died, his son Charles took over the plantation, and the young girl learned quickly from her new master that obedience was the best deterrent to beatings. But when Charles died, compromising the future of his farm, the slaves were terrified about what would happen to them. They feared the inevitable, and soon all of Charles's property and slaves were sold. Nine-year-old Isabella was ripped from the arms of her mother and sold along with a few sheep to a man she knew only as Master Neeley.

Isabella did not understand his English and struggled to obey. As a result, she endured more beatings. Each time her face was bloodied or her back burned with hot coals, she clung to her mama's words: "When you're cruelly treated, Isabella, or fall into trouble, remember to ask for God's help. He'll always hear you and help you." So she did what her mother had taught her and she prayed. But for the next two years, the beatings did not stop.

Finally, Master Neeley had had enough of the child, and in 1808, when Isabella was eleven, she was sold again, this time to another family in another New York town. They too grew exasperated with the awkward girl whose language was difficult, and they asked a local farmer named John Dumont if he wanted to purchase her. He did. And again Isabella experienced similar treatment as she had received from her previous masters where the now thirteen-year-old girl equated Master Dumont with God: both were distant authority figures who monitored everything she did though rarely seemed to hear her pleas.

Isabella spent the next seventeen years as Dumont's slave. She grew taller than most slaves, her arms and back as strong as those of some of the young men on the plantation. She was forced to marry Thomas, another Dumont slave, and she bore five children. She cooked and plowed and harvested the land so Dumont could profit from her labor. As the months and years droned on, Isabella feared she would never know anything but the evils of slavery, the agony of its monstrous pains, and the dehumanizing separation of family. She battled hopelessness, enduring the collective misery that plagued the country. After all, nothing but sorrow and hard work existed for tall, black, female slaves like her.

But in 1826, something happened. Dumont had learned that the state of New York would free its adult slaves, so he promised Isabella he would let her go early "if she would do well and be faithful." She did, but months later he reneged on his promise, claiming she hadn't been productive enough. She had tasted the possibility of freedom only to be trapped again.

This time Isabella had had enough. Perhaps she was convinced that she literally had nothing more to lose, so early one morning she gathered her youngest child, Sophia, in her arms and *walked* off the Dumont property. She did not run or even hide. She simply walked, and she kept walking until eventually she ended up at the home of a Quaker family named the Van Wagenens. They protected her and Sophia when Dumont came looking for his slaves. In fact, they offered twenty dollars for Isabella, which Dumont accepted, so she and her daughter could stay in the home of the Van Wagenens until the New York abolition law went into full effect in 1827.

While living with the Van Wagenens, Isabella learned of someone named Jesus Christ. The Quakers were kind to her and read their Holy Bible to her (Isabella remained illiterate throughout her life), and she became hungry for more. She took on the name of the Van Wagenens, as she'd done with every master before them, and felt it right as well to take on their way of life. From that moment on, she began to see a way out of the hopelessness she had endured for her entire life.

She felt hope so strongly that one day, when she was alone in their cottage, she was sure she heard a voice. Isabella got up, moved toward the fire, and listened. She turned around and again heard the soft whisper of love. In her autobiography (published in 1850), her experience is described this way:

> "Who are you?" she exclaimed, as the vision brightened into a form distinct, beaming with the beauty of holiness, and radiant with love. She then said, audibly addressing the mysterious visitant—"I know you, and I don't know you." Meaning, "You seem perfectly familiar; I feel that you not only love me, but that you always have loved me—yet I know you not—I cannot call you by name." When she said, "I know you," the subject of the vision remained distinct and quiet. When she said, "I don't know you," it moved restlessly about, like agitated waters. So while she repeated, without intermission,

"I know you, I know you," that the vision might remain—
"Who are you?" was the cry of her heart, and her whole soul
was in one deep prayer that this heavenly personage might be
revealed to her, and remain with her. At length, after bending
both soul and body with the intensity of this desire, till breath
and strength seemed failing, and she could maintain her position no longer, an answer came to her, saying distinctly, "It
is Jesus." "Yes," she responded, "it is Jesus."

Previous to these exercises of mind, she heard Jesus mentioned in reading or speaking, but had received from what she
heard no impression that he was any other than an eminent
man, like a Washington or a Lafayette. Now he appeared to her
delighted mental vision as so mild, so good, and so every way
lovely, and he loved her so much! And, how strange that he had
always loved her, and she had never known it! And how great a
blessing he conferred, in that he should stand between her and
God! And God was no longer a terror and a dread to her.[1]

At that moment, Isabella understood that this Jesus was
not just any man but one who had come to free her. She
encountered the Christ, the Living Hope, so mild and good
and lovely that life became completely new. And because
of his immediate presence in her life, she felt first her own
unworthiness and Christ's pleading on her behalf, then a
profound sense of forgiveness toward white people. "And she
felt as sensibly refreshed as when, on a hot day, an umbrella
had been interposed between her scorching head and a burning sun."[2] From that personal interaction with Jesus came
spiritual freedom for Isabella as well as a powerful sense of
purpose for proclaiming God's goodness to the world by
challenging the evils of the day.

Not long after that first introduction to Jesus Christ, Isabella prayed again, "Lord, I plan to travel up and down the
land. Thou art my last Master. Thy name is Truth and Truth
shall be my abiding name till I die."[3]

And so began the transformation of one of our country's most amazing abolitionists, advocates for equality, and

preachers of the gospel. Sojourner Truth, once a despairing and beaten slave born with all the wrong status at that time in history, was reborn into a right relationship with her maker and delivered from her oppressors. Because of her newfound love, she spent the rest of her life traveling the country, as she had promised God, devoting herself to confronting the same injustices she had endured as a slave.

She went where God took her. And that relationship led Sojourner Truth into some difficult and unbelievable circumstances. She confronted the political atrocities of the time. She spoke—in her broken English—before countless men and women in conventions, churches, courts of law, and town halls; she advised President Abraham Lincoln on resettlement, health, and education programs for African Americans and the poor; and she organized and encouraged fellow abolitionists so that society might better reflect the will of God. And years *before* the Civil War, she even sued Dumont for illegally selling her son as well as the government in Washington, DC, for discriminating against her on a train—and she won both cases! As novelist and fellow abolitionist Harriet Beecher Stowe wrote, "I do not recollect anyone who had more of that silent and subtle power which we call personal presence than this woman."[4]

Because slave owners didn't keep birth records, Sojourner Truth never knew just how old she was. But on her deathbed when she was probably in her eighties, this freed black woman—whose entire identity had been changed by Jesus Christ—reportedly said, "I'm not going to die. I'm goin' home like a shooting star."[5] And no one was likely to argue.

Enslaved by Delusion

To be sure, Isabella's story of life as a slave records one of the most shameful and agonizing aspects of American history. As an African American woman enslaved to the delusional demon of white supremacy, she brings us face-to-face with the evils inherent in every human heart. What makes her story worse, though, is the reality that for almost two centuries, slavery in America was justified, legislated, and carried out by men and women who called themselves Christians. Many slave owners, like the Dumonts, were religious, moral, and in every other way upright citizens. They were deacons in their churches, leaders in their communities, government officials in their towns. They tithed and prayed and read the Bible to their families. Some even preached to their slaves, believing that God had ordained their positions as masters to care for these "nonhuman" Africans.

But for all their "Christian" efforts, they were blinded by greed and deceived by the darkness of an institution designed and perpetuated by sin. For all their religiosity, these Christian slave owners did not seem to understand that the Christ of the Gospels hated slavery of any type—religious, economic, or physical. Somehow they never connected the biblical stories of Christ's ministry to their own situations. They missed the passages that showed Jesus not only affirming the marginalized of his culture but also setting them free. And they didn't seem to understand that he came not only to encourage the outcasts but also to include them in his life. He invited them into his family and promised to make his home in their hearts. He considered those on the fringe—slaves, women, the poor—equal with the Pharisees and religious leaders of his time. And by doing so, he defied the cultural mores of the day and paid the price in a death sentence on the cross.

Yet his crucifixion was not a surprise to him; it was his purpose. Through his sacrificial death, unholy sinners were reconciled to a holy God. And if any of his followers had missed the message, his resurrection from the dead was sure to restore their sense of hope. As Luke reported, the Son of Man came to seek and save the lost (see Luke 19:10). His kingdom had no place for the injustice of slavery, let alone slavery in the name of religious piety.

Thankfully, Isabella discovered that very truth when she met the risen Jesus. So radical was her encounter with him that her entire identity was changed, and her purpose for living redefined everything for her, even her name. From the moment of her conversion until the time she "shot home" to heaven, Sojourner Truth was devoted to only one master: Jesus. He had indeed freed her, delivering her into a new life for an entirely different kind of service.

But lest we consider her story merely an inspiring example from an admittedly dark but distant period in history, I believe it's important to recognize that many of us today are still plagued by the deception of religious rationales. It's far easier to retain the values and beliefs of religious or nationalistic traditions that we might have grown up with, even those that reinforce stereotypes and perceptions of superiority or class, than it is to encounter the living power of a man who conquered death. In other words, those "Christians" who justified enslaving the Isabellas in our nation's history were not much different from many of us modern-day citizens who believe, for example, that America is superior to other nations, that Republicans are more righteous than Democrats, that Presbyterians are more orthodox than all other denominations, or that rich, white, suburban families are more together than those in urban areas.

You get the idea. As human beings, we are each plagued by the deception of our own sins, blinded by our many delusions, and trying desperately to justify our goodness or morality, superiority, or even fear rather than walk through the hard work of repentance. We don't want to admit who we really are or just how much we fall short. As Jeremiah said in chapter 17, verse 9, "The heart is deceitful above all things and beyond cure. Who can understand it?"

So we tend to stay trapped rather than admit the depths of our depravity. Why? Because we don't really know just how lovely—and how freeing—the voice of the risen Jesus can be.

But when we do, nothing can keep us from following after him, no matter where he might take us.

The Demons of Magdala

Sojourner Truth's story parallels in some ways another story of another woman also trapped by demonic forces. She too was set free when she encountered the holy man from Galilee, and she also latched on to the hope he offered her. Just as Sojourner had been transformed by the love of Jesus, so too had Mary of Magdala been smitten by the loving freedom Jesus offered her, causing her to join his entourage as they roamed "up and down the land" around Jerusalem.

Though Mary's is one of my favorite stories in the Bible, it is also one filled with enormous pain. Yes, Mary's beautiful encounter with Jesus in the garden, recorded only in John 20:1–18, offers us an intimate glimpse into the character of our Lord. But it is beautiful primarily because we know how much tragedy Mary, like young Isabella, had been through. We know how much she had endured to get to this point with Jesus.

And how much he had endured to get to her.

As we discussed in the last chapter, Mary was one of several women who had traveled with Jesus, caring for him and his first disciples out of their own means. They were greatly attached to him. They listened to his stories and sermons, watched him feed the hungry and heal the sick, and marveled when he challenged the authorities who had previously oppressed them. Mary and the other women had grown to love this man as they had no other; after all, he had included and affirmed them in ways no other men had or would again. Something about him transcended everything she'd ever experienced.

So to have stood only a few meters from the cross when he hung dying would surely have sent Mary back into a deep sense of fear and hopelessness. She despaired, probably even to the point of fearing that the demons would come back. I imagine she couldn't help worrying what might become of her and the other women now that their master had died. Would they be separated, or even killed? Anything would seem possible for her because Mary had already encountered so much misery.

Luke tells us in chapter 8 that her hometown was Magdala, which was probably among the larger of the cities around the Sea of Galilee at the time of Jesus. It was a busy commercial area, probably a pagan center filled with markets, fish salting, and flax weaving and dyeing. Some commentators even believe that the robes worn by Jesus at the time of his trial would have been made there.

Mary grew up in this chaotic city, and some time in her life, tragedy struck. Though some believe she came from a wealthy family, we don't know exactly what that meant or what she had to endure because of it. What is clear is that Mary became enslaved not to one or two masters but to *seven* demons. Author and scholar Alice Mathews described the experience this way: "Any possessed person was an outcast from normal society. Some afflicted people were more animal than human, living in caves, roving around the countryside terrifying people with their distorted faces and wild eyes. Created by God, they were being destroyed by Satan."[6]

We don't know how long or in what cruel ways these seven demons were "destroying" Mary. They could have thrown her across hot coals, starved her for days on end, or invaded any moment of rest with screams of darkness. They would have surely separated her from any family she had as well as stripped her of any taste of spiritual hope or human dignity. She'd become a slave to evil forces she could not control, and though we can barely imagine what she endured, we do know that she was in severe bondage to these demons, desperate for deliverance and normalcy. As Eugene Peterson said, "The 'seven devils' (that possessed Mary) could refer to an utterly dissolute moral life or to an extreme form of mental illness.

Either or both of these pre-Jesus conditions, coupled with being a woman in a patriarchal society, put her at the very far edge of marginality."[7]

What is not likely is that Mary Magdalene lived like the sinful woman in Luke 7 who anointed Christ's feet with her hair. If Mary Magdalene had been a prostitute—though many have their doubts if she was—the Gospel writers would have probably included that in her "bio." Instead, we're simply told the city from which she came and what happened when Jesus found her.

And Christ responded as he always had: he took authority over the situation and commanded the demons to leave. And as Alice Mathews writes, "Deliverance must have been a life-changing liberation. Her bound spirit was set free. Her cramped limbs relaxed. Her contorted face became serene."[8]

Naturally, then, she would want to follow this man, to devote herself to him whatever that meant for her. And though Mary spent the next few years on the road with her liberator, because of the context of her past, she was hardly a credible witness for his most astonishing deed to date. Given the freedom she experienced from her bondage, how could she have been anything but utterly despairing at his death? She was a wreck. Jesus was dead.

And now on this dark morning, his body wasn't even where it was supposed to be.

Broken Hearts

It must have been sheer duty, then, that moved her to join the other women as they came to prepare the battered corpse. What must have gone through her mind as she walked down the path to say good-bye to the man who had freed her from her destitution? And what did she think when she saw the rock rolled away from the tomb?

Though each Gospel writer puts Mary and the women first at the tomb where Christ had been laid, only John provides the

detail of Mary running to get Peter and "the other disciple."
Matthew, Mark, and Luke record Mary and the other women
running to tell the disciples but as if there's no time stamp on
the story. John gives us fascinating details that take us into
the moment. When he, Peter, and Mary arrived back at the
grave and saw a tidy tomb with Christ's burial linens neatly
folded, each of the disciples had a different reaction. Peter
wandered off despondent, John looked inside at the emptiness
and believed, and Mary seemed paralyzed by despair.

Maybe enough time had passed that they'd heard the
speculation surrounding the empty tomb. What could have
happened to the body of Jesus? The stone had been rolled
away; did that mean that in spite of the guards, tomb robbers
had somehow stolen the corpse to pluck off any remaining
valuables it might have carried? If they had, did they then toss
the body into a different grave? If the body were in another
grave, how would Mary ever find him? And was she in danger
even standing there? Were robbers or thugs or guards hiding
nearby, ready also to attack or arrest her and the others?

Most of the women didn't wait around long enough to find
out. Nor did the disciples. But Mary did. Why did she stay
staring at the grave when her friends had just run off? What
did she expect would happen? What would she do next?

I think it's safe to assume that she had no more idea what
her next step would be than she knew what she was about
to encounter. So she began to cry. And as she stood there,
tears streaming down her cheeks, remembering her liberator,
something completely unexpected happened. Angels in white
appeared, and instead of falling prostrate at their presence,
Mary simply continued to weep. As anyone who's experienced such enormous loss knows, grief can overpower any
rational perspective, causing you to react in ways you later
might regret.

"Woman, why are you crying?" they asked (John 20:13).
From a human perspective, it was an amazingly insensitive
question. Why *wouldn't* she be crying? Her love was dead.

Weeping and wailing were normal responses when someone close had died, all the more when that person had been murdered before a woman's eyes. But human beings were not asking the question. These angelic beings clearly knew something she did not.

So when she heard the question, coming not from men but from the voices of angels—supernatural beings that instantly appeared in majestic glory—incredibly, Mary did not run off in terror. Nor did she drop to her knees, at least that we are told. She simply stood there weeping some more and listening.

Her grief likely clouded her thinking since she instinctively answered the angel's question with one of her own: where had they taken him, her love, the one who'd set her free? Such audacity! This formerly demon-possessed, marginalized woman dared to ask a messenger of God a question like this? Surely her broken heart had gotten the best of her. Yet maybe she, like Isabella, knew she had nothing more to lose. So she acted as if no cultural mores existed that would have otherwise prevented her from engaging in a conversation with power figures. She didn't care what she was doing. She couldn't stop the tears.

She wanted Jesus. It was cruel not to tell her where he was.

When she turned to look in another direction, she heard a different voice: "Woman, why are you crying? Who is it you are looking for?" (see v. 15).

And she did it again. She entered a conversation with another superior and expressed her most courageous but honest request yet: "Sir, if you have carried him away, tell me where you have put him, and I will get him" (v. 15). So deep was her love and devotion to the man who freed her that she was willing to risk everything in her inquiry. It was a dangerous query. For all she knew, the person she thought was a gardener was someone far worse, one who could have seized her, stolen her away, or beaten her simply because she was a woman alone in a cemetery. He could have ostracized her or condemned her—or worse. Any other man might have. Even if he had told her where the corpse was, Mary's safety would surely have been threatened once she went to retrieve it. Yes, at that moment she was more vulnerable than at perhaps any other time in her life and probably felt more alone. By now, though, it didn't matter to her. She remembered the misery of her demons, and the freedom she'd been given from them. She needed to respond.

The voice, though, was not that of a gardener, at least the kind she might have expected to meet. This man seemed good and gentle and lovely. She paused. And then she heard a beautiful sound, one she never expected to hear:

"Mary."

The voice was familiar. Like Isabella, Mary must have rubbed her eyes and thought she knew him . . . but she didn't know him. This could not be happening. This could not be real. And again, like Isabella, "At length, after bending both soul and body with the intensity of this desire, till breath and strength seemed failing, and she could maintain her position no longer, an answer came to her, saying distinctly, 'It is Jesus.' 'Yes,' she responded, 'it is Jesus.' "[9]

Yes, she *did* recognize the voice. How could it be? Jesus, the only one who could have freed her, her ultimate comfort, who'd been murdered, was standing before her. He was not the gardener or any other man. The man she'd watched die was no longer a corpse but was somehow breathing again and standing only a few feet away from her as she wept, as if his heart too had been broken. When he'd said her name—his inflection filled with a hundred intimate memories—she knew the impossible had happened. She knew *why* the tomb was empty.

Her deliverer lived.

Lessons from the Voice

At first glance, the interaction between these two is a beautiful but perplexing story. The more I think about it, the more I feel compelled to ask, why? Why did the risen Jesus appear fresh out of the grave to a desperate woman like Mary Magdalene and have his first conversation with her? Why didn't he make his grand entrance in the midst of the guards just as they were telling the news of the empty tomb to the local authorities? Surely that would have been a better publicity opportunity. And wouldn't that have eliminated all the speculation and skepticism that has spread about the empty tomb ever since?

Not likely. Instead, two things become clear from the details John recorded. First, as we know, human hearts have chosen delusions over truth throughout history. The Pharisees did not want to see Jesus alive, so even if they had, they would likely have perpetrated a number of stories about the empty tomb to keep him from stealing their power. Still, they did not deny the tomb was empty when the guards brought the news; they simply tried to keep the truth of its emptiness from getting circulated. But they certainly did not want to have to consider what a guarded but empty tomb could mean!

Second, Jesus wasn't interested in publicity. Rather, *the Son of Man came to seek and save the lost* (see Luke 19:10). Because Mary's heart had been shattered by his death, she'd felt more lost than ever. His flesh-and-blood presence once again freed her from that which threatened to hold her in bondage: Fear. Darkness. Loneliness. After all, his character and his mission throughout his time on earth had been to restore broken women and men. He hadn't changed, especially now. Mary Magdalene experienced that just as she realized *whom* the voice belonged to, which was also the first time in the story when she moved. It was as if both her paralysis and her tears had lifted. She leapt forward at the recognition, calling him by his name, "Teacher," wanting nothing more than to cling to him again so life would always be . . . safe.

But he knew her purpose far more than she did, and he wanted her to find it both in his presence and in his calling. For immediately, Jesus did what he had always done with those he loved: he sent her out to others. He comforted her, he confirmed the truth of his promise, and then he commissioned her with some very specific directions: "Go and tell my brothers that I am returning to my Father and your Father, to my God and your God" (see v. 17). It was an amazing reaffirmation of all he had ever said to her and the others, emphasizing again his invitation to an eternal relationship in which grace is always given and families are never separated.

His appearance as well as his word reinforced the truth he'd been communicating all along. Jesus chose (again) a most unlikely follower, whose heart had broken over losing him, to display his love and then to invite others to do the same. And the fact that the Gospel writers all report Mary as the first witness to the resurrection only validates the authenticity of the narrative; if they'd invented it, they would not have used pitiful women in a cemetery as their primary witnesses to the centerpiece of their faith. As we said in the last chapter, if it were fiction, it would never have been plausible.

But John's version here paints such a detailed picture of their interaction that it sounds as if Mary herself described it to him. Many scholars regard this as probable. Regardless, John writes Mary's story with such immediate images and language that the point of the passage becomes clear as we study it: he wanted to provide lasting evidence that Jesus Christ died because of his liberating love for women like Mary of Magdala. And Jesus Christ then left his grave for exactly the same reason: to make sure that women like Mary of Magdala embraced that love. As Frederick Buechner said in his book *The Faces of Jesus*, "It hardly matters how the body of Jesus came to be missing because in the last analysis what convinced the people that he had risen from the dead was not the absence of his corpse but his living presence. And so it has been ever since."[10]

Changed Again

The itinerant rabbi who had once changed Mary Magdalene, transforming her life from one of slavery to one of freedom, continued the good work he began in her during that early morning encounter in the garden. When he died on the cross and hope died in her heart, he heard her cries. And when she stood completely and utterly at the end of her humanity, staring at a tomb where there was supposed to be a corpse, her heart—and his—broke again. It was in this breaking that she was visited, not only by ministering angels but by Jesus Christ himself. In other words, as she stood helpless, paralyzed, and alone, he came near. He comforted the despairing woman with words of belonging and hope, a clear voice she heard proclaiming to her: "I am returning to my Father and your Father, my God and your God" (John 20:17).

And he comforts still.

For hearing his voice was the moment Mary Magdalene's entire world changed. That was when she finally saw what he had been trying to show her all along: that nothing could stop him from loving those on the margins, the poor or outcasts or women . . . like her. Not political powers, not evil institutions, not torture or execution, not even death could keep him from his ultimate prize: her.

You. Me. Us.

He stood before her literally as the living proof she would need to carry on in her faith. Yes, she had believed she would never again see the man who had freed her from evil. But he was greater than her belief, for now she was watching him walk in a garden near a tomb. She was listening to his voice as he spoke her name.

And when he spoke, she was confronted with a truth that was humanly impossible. There was no mistaking: she was hearing the same voice that had once commanded the demons to leave her, now calling her to a new reality, a new identity, a new purpose. Her faith before had been in his physical presence; now she realized there was a power far greater than flesh and blood, something so real and so eternal that she would never again have to fear slavery to anything but this loving master.

It was the power of his voice, his Word, his presence that would sustain her—and those who believed her story—through whatever circumstances she might face.

That morning, Mary went from absolute sorrow to astonishing joy. She'd been paralyzed by grief and despair and now was transformed by the miracle standing before her, reminding her that their relationship was hardly over. It had only begun! The Presence of Love was with her, as it is with us, affirming the message he'd proclaimed from the start: God still pursues wounded, frightened women and men, loves them back to health, and instills in them a purpose and a freedom that challenges the darkness around us with the light of life. Indeed, it frees us to be who he's created us to be.

And when we hear the truth of *that* voice, we can be sure he'll take us like a sojourner "up and down the land" until, eventually, he calls us home like a shooting star.

IN-BETWEEN REFLECTION

1. What issues or truths surfaced as you read Isabella's story?
2. Why do you think Sojourner Truth chose a name like that? What spiritual name might characterize your mission and life?
3. Mary Magdalene had been enslaved as well. What do you think her life had been like before Jesus freed her, and why do you think that would be important to understand in our contemporary culture? How do you think our culture might be enslaved to delusions or deceptions? How can we respond?
4. Review John 20:3–11. Notice that when Mary first arrived at the tomb, John recorded the detail that she then ran to get Peter and the "other disciple" before running back. Each then responded differently to the empty and

tidy tomb. What do you think would have gone through your mind? Which of the three do you best relate to and why?

5. What does this chapter teach you about words like freedom, purpose, justice, and truth?

PRAYER:

May your truth, dear Lord, always lead me, giving me courage to admit my helplessness and cry out to you for change. Thank you that you still offer your presence as our comfort. Amen.

PREPARATION

Please take a few moments right now to read Luke 24:13–35 printed below. It is another account recorded in Scripture of Christ encountering his friends after he'd died. Once you've read it, pause for a quiet moment to consider the words you've read.

LUKE 24:13–35

Now that same day two of them were going to a village called Emmaus, about seven miles from Jerusalem. They were talking with each other about everything that had happened. As they talked and discussed these things with each other, Jesus himself came up and walked along with them; but they were kept from recognizing him.

He asked them, "What are you discussing together as you walk along?"

They stood still, their faces downcast. One of them, named Cleopas, asked him, "Are you only a visitor to Jerusalem and do not know the things that have happened there in these days?"

"What things?" he asked.

"About Jesus of Nazareth," they replied. "He was a prophet, powerful in word and deed before God and all the people. The chief priests and our rulers handed him over to be sentenced to death, and they crucified him; but we had hoped that he was the one who was going to redeem Israel. And what is more, it is the third day since all this took place. In addition, some of our women amazed us. They went to the tomb early this morning but didn't find his body. They came and told us that they had seen a vision of angels, who said he was alive. Then some of our companions went to the tomb and found it just as the women had said, but him they did not see."

He said to them, "How foolish you are, and how slow of heart to believe all that the prophets have spoken! Did not the Christ have to suffer these things and then enter his glory?" And beginning with Moses and all the Prophets, he explained to them what was said in all the Scriptures concerning himself.

As they approached the village to which they were going, Jesus acted as if he were going farther. But they urged him strongly, "Stay with us, for it is nearly evening; the day is almost over." So he went in to stay with them.

When he was at the table with them, he took bread, gave thanks, broke it and began to give it to them. Then their eyes were opened and they recognized him, and he disappeared from their sight. They asked each other, "Were not our hearts burning within us while he talked with us on the road and opened the Scriptures to us?"

They got up and returned at once to Jerusalem. There they found the Eleven and those with them, assembled together and saying, "It is true! The Lord has risen and has appeared to Simon." Then the two told what had happened on the way, and how Jesus was recognized by them when he broke the bread.

When you are ready, continue reflecting on the following question:

Perhaps you've read this story before. What new insights or observations did you notice as you read about the encounter on the Emmaus Road? Jot them down. Take a few moments to reflect before reading the next chapter.

PRAYER:

Thank you, Jesus, that you are the Word made flesh and the fulfillment of the Scriptures. Please help me to see the Bible as a gift for the ages and not take it for granted. Amen.

4

Teachable Moments

We walked two by two across the campus, robed in red or blue or black regalia. Mortarboards sat awkwardly across our heads, tassels dangling near our eyes. Two professors in front of me traded friendly banter while two behind me caught up on summer vacations. I exchanged small talk with my walking partner until we came to the edge of a massive red brick building. We waited at the foot of the steps, a late summer breeze whisking across our faces, until a formal procession began. I looked up. The white steeple towering over us symbolized the direction we as a Christian community were to look. After all, this was a corporate celebration, one meant to provide perspective and inspiration for a new academic year.

Then I heard organ music. Its notes pulled us up the steps, through the doors, and down a long aisle that separated rows and rows of pews. This morning, the pews were lined with hundreds of college students standing as we entered, their eyes wide as we marched past them to several rows of pews and chairs near the front of the chapel. We joined voices in song until a white-haired leader stood behind a podium on the stage, smiled, and welcomed us to the college's first official ceremony of the new academic year.

For the next fifty minutes or so, prayers were offered, Scriptures were read, hymns were sung, and wisdom was imparted. Each nurtured a vision for the tasks before us while turning our souls toward God for his help. This tradition was established long ago at colleges across the country, preceding even this school with its 120-year history in Massachusetts. Gordon College, the small liberal arts college where I had just begun working, was in many ways like other institutions of higher learning: its heritage was based on Jesus Christ.

Academic communities from Harvard, Yale, and Princeton to Columbia, Brown, and Dartmouth all trace their roots to a mission to educate young people in the light of God's Word. The proof is not only in their archives but also in their Latin mottos, most of which are prominently engraved on buildings you can still see today across any of their campuses. Columbia, for instance, which was founded by Episcopalians, set as its mission, *"In lumine Tuo videbimus lumen,"* or "In Thy light shall we see the light." Presbyterians created Princeton with the core belief that *"Dei sub numine viget,"* or "Under God's power she flourishes." Baptists started Brown with the acknowledgment that *"In Deo speramus,"* or "In God we hope." And Congregationalists founded both Harvard, the country's oldest university, whose mission was its motto, *"Veritas Christo et Ecclesiae,"* or "Truth for Christ and the Church," and Dartmouth, who might have anticipated the difficult days ahead by choosing a passage about John the Baptist as its motto: *"Vox clamantis in deserto,"* or "A voice crying in the wilderness."

Universities like these once honored the start—and the gift—of another academic year with convocation services like Gordon's. They too had viewed as their core mission the spiritual education of the next generation, primarily because their leaders had believed the fundamental truths of

Christianity. Bible study had been a daily requirement and theology and ministry courses "strongly encouraged" in each Ivy League institution. But somewhere along the road, the focus on Christian faith in these colleges shifted. Their vision moved. Their values changed.

Little wonder. Education has a way of testing and shaping what you believe. That is its entire purpose. By nature, education is a process that often means wrestling hard with new ideas or dissecting old ones. Good classrooms become incubators for creative discovery and thoughtful consideration of their varied subjects. Better classrooms help learners explore new ground while reinforcing the reality that "all truth is God's truth."

So it isn't difficult to see how leaders of Ivy League institutions began forgetting their original purposes. The cultural excitement of competing ideas must have been hard to resist. The times were changing, and students and professors alike were becoming more and more interested in subjects to which they did not easily find sacred or holy connections. Especially as the country became increasingly industrialized, the Harvards of the US went through a series of spiritual crises. Man and his "enlightened" sense of progress gradually replaced God as the center and purpose of an Ivy League education, resulting in today's biblically barren halls where Christianity is often dismissed as irrelevant to intellectual pursuits.

I can't blame them. Who of us has not gone through our own disappointment or disillusionment or crisis of faith when put to the test? Who hasn't wrestled hard with ideas that seemed counter to the beliefs we might have grown up with? And what is learning and growing as a Christian if not a constant state of personal changes?

My own experience confirms this. Most who knew me thirty years ago would probably have laughed if they'd seen me that morning in convocation or discovered I now teach and write at a Christian college. I had been a terrible student as an undergraduate at a state university, just as anxious and eager to end my time there as I had been to start it. I knew I'd been expected to go to college, but as an insecure eighteen-year-old, I really had no idea what that would require of me. I was more interested in finding friends or playing soccer than in any academic pursuit. Classes, textbooks, exams, and papers often seemed over my head, leaving me discouraged or distracted from the real experiences I thought I needed to prepare me for a career as a high school teacher. I managed to pass most classes, but barely.

By age twenty-one, I had heard the story of Jesus Christ and responded with a new Christian faith. Suddenly, college life seemed to have more focus. I began to take my education more seriously, which meant I began asking more questions (and showing up to more classes). I wanted to understand the way Jesus related to the courses I was studying, if he did at all. I assumed somehow that he did, but I had no idea how. Even after a short visit at a small Christian college, I didn't seem to have the tools for making sense of the ideas and gifts I had for a career in education.

But, eventually, my purpose for studying became clearer. I needed to graduate from college if I wanted to get a job teaching at a high school. Period. If I didn't have a diploma, I wouldn't be considered for any position, especially at a time when many professors warned me our country had too many teachers. The competition would be fierce. And even if I did manage to graduate with a degree in education, it wouldn't be easy to land a job, they'd say, with an academic record like mine. It was hard to resist the latest cultural paranoia.

Yet in spite of those embarrassingly bad years as a student or the surplus of secondary teachers or even the warnings from those older and wiser, four months after I graduated from college I *was* hired to teach at a suburban high school in Colorado. In fact, since then, I have ironically watched a career in education take form. From those challenging days at a high school, I have worked on several college campuses, taught writing and communication classes in classrooms and retreats, and worked as a journalist for various publications on issues related to education. I've even been employed as a writer at one of those Ivy League schools that today likes to call itself a "world-class institution." And quite miraculously, I've earned two more degrees.

Still, in spite of all these experiences, only when I began to study the Bible on my own and with friends—*really study it*—did a foundation for work and education start to take root. And then only as I began listening week after week to the sermons of a gifted pastor at a local church did I see a framework built upon that foundation. Both taught me what some of those Ivy League scholars might have forgotten: that the ministry, death, and life of Jesus Christ *did* indeed have implications for every subject I had studied (and taught) in college and for every job I'd been offered (and taken). So much so that years later I continue to see that the value and power of an education founded not on the ideals or values of Christianity but on the living person of Jesus himself, our ultimate teacher and shepherd, transcends any cultural fad. It's an education that lasts for eternity.

Which was how—and why—I arrived at Gordon College. Across its campus, its heritage can still be seen in its buildings and in its community. Its story goes like this: during the mid-1800s, Adoniram Judson Gordon saw the same trends across the country as his fellow educators at Harvard and Yale and even his alma mater, Brown University. He knew how important higher education was. But because of his vibrant relationship with Christ, he also believed that *how* a person learned could make a lasting impact on the world. So in 1889 he started a missionary training institute in Boston with a global vision, immediately enrolling not just young white men but African Americans and women as well. The college grew not away from Jesus but toward him, and soon it blended biblical and theological training with a full liberal arts education that today still acknowledges learning as a gift from God. In every classroom here, Jesus is relevant to the hard academic wrestling students and professors do together that defines their academic lives.

And Gordon College is not alone. As part of the Council of Christian Colleges and Universities, it is one of over 120 member academic institutions throughout the world that remain committed to the spiritual education of the next generation, anchored not on ideals but on Christ himself. As a result, thousands of young people today are entering their careers with a Christ-centered foundation laid and built by some of the smartest—and godliest—people I've ever met.

Thankfully, this movement has happened because Christian educators like A. J. Gordon knew the impact young people could have on the world. Gordon himself discovered it early on in his own ministry when he came across a poem written in 1864 by a sixteen-year-old Canadian named William R. Featherstone. Gordon was cut to the quick by its power and immediately resonated with its personal sense of mission. Featherstone's poem was a response to having just met the living Jesus. When Gordon read it, he put it to music, creating one of the most beautiful hymns congregations across denominations use to this day.

And it was this hymn that the organist played that first fall convocation I began working at his namesake college, a hymn that has become as much a tradition as convocation itself each time Gordon College ushers in a new academic year. And in many ways, its lyrics still reflect the mission of the vibrant place of education:

> My Jesus, I love Thee, I know Thou art mine;
> For Thee all the follies of sin I resign.
> My gracious Redeemer, my Savior art Thou;
> If ever I loved Thee, my Jesus, 'tis now.
>
> I love Thee because Thou has first loved me,
> And purchased my pardon on Calvary's tree.

I love Thee for wearing the thorns on Thy brow;
If ever I loved Thee, my Jesus, 'tis now.

I'll love Thee in life, I will love Thee in death,
And praise Thee as long as Thou lendest me breath;
And say when the death dew lies cold on my brow,
If ever I loved Thee, my Jesus, 'tis now.

In mansions of glory and endless delight,
I'll ever adore Thee in heaven so bright;
I'll sing with the glittering crown on my brow;
If ever I loved Thee, my Jesus, 'tis now.

Looking toward Emmaus

Obviously, the story of education in the United States has been shaped by a variety of influences and reflects what can happen when universities ignore—or affirm—the truth of Jesus Christ. Entire sectors of culture can be affected as students leave the halls of academia to become leaders in their fields. The ripple effect on a society is as visible as the Latin mottos on Ivy League campuses.

This is why I have always been encouraged by the reality that so many great contributions to the world's betterment have been made by Christians who acknowledge a risen Jesus. Of course, many tragedies have been perpetrated in the name of religion. But many positive advances have been made in fields such as music, science, art, journalism, politics, technology, and medicine by faithful followers of the risen Lord. These women and men recognized that Christ's daily and real presence was not a side note to their careers but the very reason for it. At the center of their faith has always been a *book* from which they've renewed their minds and sharpened their vision. And they have always had a Teacher who has made a habit of personally guiding his "students" through some of history's most difficult periods. He has not changed with the times.

Consequently, their collective and powerful responses to the living person of Jesus Christ encourage us in our various callings whenever we feel tested to believe otherwise. As Saint Augustine of Hippo wrote, "I have read in Plato and Cicero sayings that are wise and very beautiful; but I have never read in either of them: Come unto me all ye that labor and are heavy laden."

It is thrilling for me then as a teacher to come to this story in Luke 24:13–35, one of the most famous educational exchanges in all of Scripture. The story of Jesus and the two people on the road to Emmaus is a glimpse of the best kind of learning imaginable: personal, interactive, and grounded in Scripture. It is a fantastically teachable moment.

At first glance, though, it seemed like just a couple of folks out for a hurried walk, trying to make sense of an immensely disappointing experience. They were surprised to bump into a stranger who seemed so out of the loop. When they tried to explain to him what had happened, to enlighten the stranger with their admittedly limited understanding of the recent events, he turned the conversation in a completely unexpected direction. He asked them questions and then gave them the lecture of a lifetime, one that was so satisfying and so stimulating they didn't want it to end.

That simple but profound exchange has today made the Emmaus road famous, even turning it into a popular symbol within many contemporary circles. In fact, it's developed an enormously positive image, making it, in marketing terms, a hip and inviting brand. It's got legs, as they say. And an Internet search confirms it, yielding hundreds of results. Emmaus Road, for instance, is also the name of a Christian rock band. Several churches across the country, as well as intentional Christian communities, have claimed its name as both their mission and their motto. But there's also an Emmaus Road movie review website, several schools and ministries named the Emmaus Road, an Emmaus Road publishing company, and even an Emmaus Road gospel quartet, to list only a few.

What is it about the Emmaus road that makes it such an endearing story on so many levels, one so many people today want to identify with? Why does a rather uneventful tale of a simple walk continue to draw us in, offering rich material for countless sermons and classroom lessons?

And why does the resurrected Jesus make his second appearance from the dead to two people we've barely heard of?

Walking Back Home

It had been a bad week. Like two college students who had just dropped out of school, Cleopas and his companion were heading away from defeat. Their heads were hanging low and their conversation must have been heavy with pity and despair. Once again they must have been asking the hard questions of what to do with their future. They had expected so much more from their teacher, from the bright young rabbi who had inspired them, helped them believe things could be different in Jerusalem, and motivated them to discover a new way of thinking about life. He had been powerful in word and deed, enough so for them to invest their whole lives in what he said.

But when the local authorities dismissed his ideas and arrested him for his radical claims, the two began to second-guess themselves. A few days later when the teacher was sentenced to death, they were utterly devastated. It grew worse when some of their friends that very morning had begun hallucinating about the tomb where his corpse had been laid, talking as if he hadn't really died. Now Cleopas and his friend just wanted out. It was all too confusing and too discouraging. Their heads were spinning from the week's events; the news they'd heard earlier that morning only made things worse.

So they headed home to Emmaus. With its name derived from the Hebrew word *hammat*, or "hot spring," Emmaus was a village located about seven miles from Jerusalem. The road was busy with merchants and travelers coming and going between the two towns. Cleopas, whose name meant "of a renowned father," could have also been the Clopas John wrote about later in John 19:25, where he is identified as the husband of another Mary who had been present at Christ's crucifixion. That Clopas became the father of Simeon, who later became a head of the church in Jerusalem. But while commentators are not certain if the two were the same person, what they do agree on about the Cleopas of the Emmaus road was that his name was common, like Joe or Bill. He could have been any Cleopas who had loved listening to the teacher's lectures. And the same is true about his companion. Though some people think the companion was in fact his wife, her identity—if it was a "her"—remains unclear.

One thing was clear, though, about these two students of Jesus: they were not of the inner circle of Christ's disciples. They were not mentioned earlier in other passages when the disciples' names were listed. Nor were they mentioned later as leaders of the early church in the book of Acts. We're not sure even if they graduated after those early tests when they wrestled with just what to believe, or for that matter, who to believe.

They were simply lay folks. Common. Ordinary. Walking home after a horrendous week, probably because they didn't know what else to do and because they didn't have a good enough reason to stay in Jerusalem. They'd left the disciples and their other new friends and headed quickly out of town. Apparently they were not walking too fast, though, since Jesus, traveling for some reason in the same direction, overtook them. He bent his ear in their direction, eavesdropped on their conversation, and was intrigued enough by what he was hearing that he slowed his pace to walk alongside them.

Then he dared them with a question, though I suspect he already knew the answer. He asked them what they were talking about, and his question literally stopped them in their tracks. "They stood still, their faces downcast," Luke wrote of their response (24:17). The Greek suggests a look of gloom or sadness—sullen, dark. They must have exchanged glances when they heard the question, trying to figure out two things: how they could broach the subject with a stranger while casually walking along a busy road, and why he didn't know in the first place.

How could someone not have heard about the young rabbi who'd been crucified? Cleopas asked. The news had spread throughout the town, not in the headlines or on television but from neighbor to neighbor. Only a visitor to Jerusalem could have remained unaware, he said. And Cleopas was partially right about that; the man before them *was* a visitor of sorts.

These two had expected their rabbi to be so much more. They knew their spiritual history well enough that they had come to believe the long-awaited Messiah would be the one who would bring about a military redemption and set Israel free from Roman occupation. He was the one who'd redeem Israel from her enemies and set up the kingdom of God anew. These things he would do, they thought.

Except Jesus their Messiah was dead. And so the kind of redemption they expected was impossible. Before his death, they'd been hopeful their circumstances would change. Now the one they thought might be able to change everything had been murdered. They'd believed one thing about him, but quite another had happened. Recounting it all again to this stranger didn't help. They were confused. Numb. Confounded.

They might have been on the road to Emmaus, but they did not know where their lives were headed.

Intellectual Wrestling

Their leader had died. They were heading home, leaving their new community and lifestyle, still raw with the pain of disillusionment and worried about having been associated with the young rabbi in the first place. It was a frightening moment.

Except for one thing. As Eugene Peterson put it, "The Emmaus-bound pair had no idea that the person they were talking to was also the person they were talking about. They were in the presence of resurrection, walking 'in the land of the living,' and they didn't know it."[1]

Why would they? There was no precedent for dead teachers coming alive again, no history of murdered leaders ever reappearing in flesh and blood to continue inspiring them. Besides, even if something so impossible were to have happened, wouldn't a good teacher have picked the brightest students of the class to visit? Wouldn't he have chosen better, more intellectually astute students before whom to make such a strange but important appearance, one that had the potential to change the world, one that might just become the anchor for community traditions throughout the ages?

Surely he shouldn't have selected a couple of mediocre students already absorbed by a sense of defeat and panic, both of which pretty well defined Cleopas and his companion. These two were lost and afraid, aware of the dangers and alienation they now faced without a core belief or a community to guide them. Their teacher was gone; they had no support system in place and no plans for the future. The culture was against them. Why would they think anything would be different?

I suspect the last thing these two expected was a really good lecture as they walked along the road, preceded first by a strong rebuke. "How foolish you are, and how slow of heart to believe all that the prophets have spoken!" (Luke 24:25). Was the stranger being cruel? Or perhaps the teacher was reestablishing his authority? Was he doing what all master teachers have done since—getting the attention of his pupils with a personal challenge?

Whatever his strategy, it worked. What ensued must have been an amazing discourse, a lecture that thousands of theologians and Bible scholars have tried to piece together ever since. Jesus recalled how story after story in the Scriptures from Genesis to the Minor Prophets signaled his arrival. Whether he recounted Moses leading the people through the Red Sea or how Daniel's friends survived the fiery furnace, Jesus showed them that the Son of Man had been present throughout the ages. How time and again, the people of God had lost their way, falling into exile because the cultural trends were too hard to resist, yet they were pursued nonetheless and rescued by the sacrificial hand of the Almighty. The narrative of the Old Testament confirmed such themes on each page, each time pointing to the reality that God would provide a way out. A rescue plan. A deliverer. I like how my friend Sally Lloyd Jones put it in her beautiful children's book *The Jesus Storybook Bible*: "Every story whispers His Name."

There in the middle of the Emmaus road, Jesus whispered. He reminded these two fearful souls that God's work had always been about this moment, that it had always been pointing to the time when the Son of Man would come to earth, offer himself for their sake, and then enter his glory. How many times had he told them before? Yes, the Son of Man must suffer; he'd said it over and over, and Luke recorded it in 9:22 and 17:25.

Yet in spite of the impending demise he invited every time he had made such a claim, despite the stakes being raised every time he publicly acknowledged his purpose, Jesus had always been confirming the story that Israel's Scriptures had been telling all along. He was—and is—the Messiah.

Cleopas and friend had been absorbed by the despair of their circumstances, but Christ singled them out on only his second appearance to challenge their thinking. How? Not only by reviewing for them the biblical accounts of the past but also by offering them his once dead, now alive presence *at that moment*. They might have felt as vulnerable and raw as Mary had earlier that day. And yet he responded to them uniquely, according to their need, not by saying their names as he had with Mary but by recounting the truth of Scripture so they could hear it from his voice to their own ears.

The Scripture *had* been fulfilled after all. And he was standing before them.

Why then didn't they recognize him as he spoke?

Lessons Learned

Though modern minds might still struggle with the historical evidence of the Emmaus road and others might want to sentimentalize it by suggesting that "Jesus is with us in thought," I believe Luke recorded it for a purpose. He acted as a careful journalist first, reporting what had happened as two more unlikely witnesses recounted this astounding event to the other disciples later that night.

Some commentators compare this story to that of another despairing couple who "lost" Jesus during the Passover (see Luke 2:41–52). Mary and Joseph had hurried back to the city, completely beside themselves because they could not find their son. They had searched in vain for three days until finally they stumbled on him in the temple, where he told them he had to be about his father's business. Both couples were tired, anxious, desperate.

On the Emmaus road, Cleopas and his companion, confused by what they'd seen and heard, were now listening to a stranger give them hard words. He told them it had been necessary for the Messiah "to suffer these things and then enter his glory" (Luke 24:26). Both in the temple as a boy and now on the Emmaus road as a resurrected man, he knew the urgency of his mission.

No matter what it cost him, he was confirming again and again the truth of Scripture and of his kingdom. He was fulfilling God's plan as the confirmation of the Word made flesh, just as he fulfilled the deepest needs of those he visited—and still visits.

But by confirming who he was, he also confronted the combined cultural, spiritual, and political powers of the world (Herod, Caesar, Pilate, Satan, sin) to announce that his kingdom would be one of truth and mercy and community, one that would affect every aspect of their lives. Eugene Peterson described it best: "As the Emmaus pilgrims listened to Jesus expounding on the Scriptures that day, they realized that they weren't dealing with the latest thing but with the oldest thing. They were, as we say, 'getting the picture.' "[2]

Still, no matter how grand the "picture" was, they did not recognize him as they listened. Yes, they were utterly fascinated by what he said, so much so that they didn't want him to stop. In fact, they asked him to join them for dinner in their home, just so he could keep talking and they could keep listening. But Luke gives a funny little detail in verse 16: that there on the Emmaus road, when he was poring over Scripture, "they were kept from recognizing him," as if some divine intervention had intentionally prevented them from understanding who he was.

Perhaps they couldn't have handled the extreme emotional shift if they had recognized him. Perhaps it would have been too much. My husband put it like this: "Imagine if they *weren't* kept from recognizing him! They'd have been like eager puppy dogs, falling over themselves with excitement, wanting to run out and tell everyone immediately, *but the teachable moment would have been be lost.*"

As it was, the teachable moment was deep and rich, and Jesus himself explained to them who he was in a way that they would be able to come back to time and again for the rest of their lives, to reproduce and draw from for the days ahead. They were in fact given the best, most accurate biblical and theological lesson possible in the space of a long walk, from the Messiah himself! They had been eager to reconcile the events of the crucifixion with the bizarre account they'd heard earlier of his reported resurrection. They wanted to make sense of the teaching and the life they had experienced with Jesus, even if his death had sent them into depression.

So the wisdom of keeping them from recognizing him was well proven. For when did they recognize him? When he broke bread, their eyes were opened. They remembered why he had seemed familiar. And as soon as they *saw* him, he disappeared, proving the value of learning to understand something—in God's time.

Because what did they do next? They *did* fall all over themselves like puppies. They jumped up from the table and immediately ran back seven miles—in the dark—to the friends they'd just left.

Converted by Truth

Their spiritual eyes had not been opened when they heard Christ unpack the Scriptures. Though their hearts were burning then, they were not changed, as if the lecture alone could transform them from despair to hope. Studying the Bible as an academic exercise was not the point, as helpful as it was in building a lasting foundation.

No, they were changed when they invited him into their home and participated with him in an act much like the one he'd shared with his disciples on the night before his death. It was this reminder they needed to feed on—this reality that death had indeed come to their Lord but his life was stronger than all the forces of the world combined.

Still, I have to wonder, why tell that to these two? They were hardly the leaders of a revolution. They had left the community of fellow believers because they didn't know what else to do. And yet Jesus, the Good Shepherd, went in search of the lost sheep and sent them back to the flock. Like Mary, who might have been in danger of relapse, these two were heading back to their own lives, away from the others, pushed out to the fringe. They were unsettled about what had happened. They were even calling it quits.

Why didn't Jesus deliver one of his most powerful lectures to Peter or John? Why not unpack the Scriptures to those leaders who were likely going to be leading the first church, laying the foundation for all those coming after? Why give the greatest biblical history lesson ever recorded in ancient literature to these two no-names, these two laypeople who didn't even recognize him? How odd that he would appear in his risen glory to these on the "lower" rung of the spiritual ladder.

Except that those who were on the margins were always his priority.

In crisis, he responded in priority of need. As the resurrected Christ but still a man, he couldn't be with all of them at the same time; that would come later, at his ascension, when he sent the Holy Spirit to those who would receive him for all time. Instead, Jesus had to make choices as a flesh-and-blood man, which might have meant he had to consider who needed him most at that time. These two were genuinely wrestling with the terrible and bizarre news they'd learned. They were stuck in their despair. Their hearts were broken with sorrow.

They needed a broken reed, one bruised for their transgressions, a man familiar with sorrow and grief (Isa. 53:2–3). As Frederick Buechner beautifully described it, "It was only when he blessed the bread and then broke it and gave it to them that they saw who he was. They could hardly see the face of the stranger for the great sunflower of light that suddenly blossomed out behind it, but they saw enough to know that it was not a stranger who was standing there."[3]

And once they realized just who it had been at their table, they did not waste a second. They ran seven miles back to Jerusalem during the night to tell the others about the man who'd suffered in death and who indeed had risen from the grave *for them*. They immediately responded to the good news by wanting to share the Good News!

I have often wondered if Jesus appeared to Cleopas and his companion for the same reason we need him to appear to us today: we live and walk around as if he's dead. We live as if our greatest hope and truest love somehow died and left us alone, left us to fend for ourselves. As with these two, so, too, do our doubts often overtake us as the circumstances of life become too hard or too painful to keep going. As with Cleopas and friend, so, too, do we need to encounter the living Word anew so that our sorrow may turn to joy and our despair to hope.

Until we do, our Christianity is simply an intellectual experience or a value system we try to live up to. Because we are not converted or changed when we merely consider the claims of Christ or even stand at the cross watching him die. Yet if we focus only on the resurrection we forget the sacrifice he made. We need both each time we walk out the door and down whatever road we're called to take.

His resurrected presence after his crucified death anchors us for whatever circumstances we face; it is our daily confirmation of truth and the help we need to make sense of a world that is often confusing. This two-sided truth—Christ's sacrificial death *and* his resurrection—keeps us from going adrift.

But life with him—as it was that day with Cleopas and his friend—is never just about us. They got up from their cozy home and returned *at once* to Jerusalem, where they found the disciples. They didn't stop to think about what they were doing. They just found their friends because they could not resist telling them what they knew intellectually sounded absurd: "It is true! The Lord has risen" (Luke 24:34).

Their words have echoed through the halls of many chapels and classrooms ever since. This single truth of the Risen Lord has been the driving force behind more lessons, classrooms, and convocations, more personal careers and cultural changes than any other in the history of the Western world.

What better reason, then, to sing hymns at the start of a school year?

IN-BETWEEN REFLECTION

1. Recall a time when a teacher or a class (in high school, college, or a local church) inspired you in an entirely new way. What made the difference for you?

2. Why do you think Jesus chose these two to hear one of history's most amazing lectures on God's pursuit of his people throughout the Bible?

3. Where are you now on your own Emmaus road? Are you on your way back to the familiar out of fear or weariness? Or are you wanting to listen to God's Word? Sitting at the table, inviting Jesus in for a meal? Returning to others with new purpose? Or somewhere else? (Note: there is no wrong place on the road. We're *all* in process!)

4. Why do you think Cleopas and his friend recognized Jesus when he broke bread? What does that signal to you about how he communicates to us today?

5. Pause for a moment to reflect on the words to the hymn "My Jesus, I Love Thee." If you know the melody, perhaps you'd like to take a moment of worship to sing the hymn as a prayer.

PRAYER:

Thank you, Almighty God, that your Son, the Word made flesh, purchased my pardon on Calvary's tree and renews my mind daily in eternal truth. If ever I loved thee, my Jesus, 'tis now. Amen.

--- PREPARATION ---

Please take a few moments right now to read Luke 24:34–49 and John 20:19–23, printed below. They are accounts recorded in Scripture of the Risen Christ encountering his friends in the upper room. Once you've read them, pause for a quiet moment to consider the words you've read.

LUKE 24:34–49

"It is true! The Lord has risen and has appeared to Simon." Then the two told what had happened on the way, and how Jesus was recognized by them when he broke the bread.

While they were still talking about this, Jesus himself stood among them and said to them, "Peace be with you."

They were startled and frightened, thinking they saw a ghost. He said to them, "Why are you troubled, and why do doubts rise in your minds? Look at my hands and my feet. It is I myself! Touch me and see; a ghost does not have flesh and bones, as you see I have."

When he had said this, he showed them his hands and feet. And while they still did not believe it because of joy and amazement, he asked them, "Do you have anything here to eat?" They gave him a piece of broiled fish, and he took it and ate it in their presence.

He said to them, "This is what I told you while I was still with you: Everything must be fulfilled that is written about me in the Law of Moses, the Prophets and the Psalms."

Then he opened their minds so they could understand the Scriptures. He told them, "This is what is written: The Christ will suffer and rise from the dead on the third day, and repentance and forgiveness of sins will be preached in his name to all nations, beginning at Jerusalem. You are witnesses of these things. I am going to send you what my Father has promised; but stay in the city until you have been clothed with power from on high."

JOHN 20:19–23

On the evening of that first day of the week, when the disciples were together, with the doors locked for fear of the Jews, Jesus came and stood among them and said, "Peace be with you!" After he said this, he showed them his hands and side. The disciples were overjoyed when they saw the Lord.

Again Jesus said, "Peace be with you! As the Father has sent me, I am sending you." And with that he breathed on them and said, "Receive the Holy Spirit. If you forgive anyone his sins, they are forgiven; if you do not forgive them, they are not forgiven."

When you are ready, continue reflecting on the following question:

Perhaps you've read this story before. What new insights or observations did you notice as you read this story in both Gospel accounts? Jot them down. Take a few moments to reflect before reading the next chapter.

PRAYER:

Your presence and your Word, dear Lord, are my peace and my comfort. Amen.

5

Sensory Appeal

On a crisp fall day in 1998, a classroom of fifth-grade students gathered in a drafty room and stared. The girls and boys had come from their Boston elementary school for a different sort of field trip, visiting not a circus or a planetarium or a zoo but an old house on the Fenway (Park), a mansion really. When they arrived, they were directed toward a large image full of colors, creatures, and seas. They were told to sit and to stare long and hard at the picture before them. And so they did. Wiggling on the floor, sniffling, scratching their heads, trying with all the ten-year-old concentration they could muster to make sense of an admittedly weird scene in front of them.

What they saw was a nearly six-by-seven-foot canvas depicting the story of a Phoenician princess being carried off into the sky by a white bull, symbolizing the mythological tale of the Greek god Zeus capturing Europa, a lovely but terrified female mortal. Europa—a large woman, pale breast and legs exposed—holds a flowing red scarf in one hand and the horn of the bull in the other as chubby angel-like beings surround her. In the distance, the sea meets a mountain, and sailors or friends barely recognizable gather on the shore to watch as Europa is taken away, blue sky above them. The clouds above Europa, though, are dark, and her face is shadowed in fear.

Titian's *Europa* was painted sometime between 1575 and 1580. Tiziano Vecellio (also known as Titian), one of the most influential Italian artists of the Renaissance tradition, painted *Europa* during the latter part of his life, years after he had depicted biblical themes in his paintings, such as a three-tier *Assumption of the Virgin (Mary)*, the largest altarpiece in Venice, located today in the Basilica of Santa Maria Gloriosa dei Frari. *Europa*, however, is considered one of his masterpieces from that tradition; it includes both broad and delicate brush strokes, textured colors of reds and pinks and blues, and a complement of images that give the painting a sense of motion, as if the princess is mid-flight and you too are in the sky, watching helplessly as she is led away.

Why were these urban children staring at a painting almost 450 years old? And why in a drafty old room of a hundred-year-old mansion? The answer was simple and most intriguing: another artist—a contemporary musician named Kenneth Frazelle, to be exact—wanted to know what these children *heard* as they looked at the painting.

The year before, Frazelle, a gifted American composer, had accepted an artist in residency position at the Isabella Stewart Gardner Museum in Boston, one of New England's most interesting museums of art, which has also become a favorite of mine. Frazelle wondered what might happen if he invited a group of neighboring fifth-graders—whose school partners with the museum's education program—to describe what they *heard* when they stared at the painting. The musician chose Titian's sixteenth-century masterpiece *Europa* as their "textbook" because of its place as a standard in art history and the dramatic scene it portrays. But mostly he was curious how they might respond since he himself often *saw* music when he looked at great paintings or images. In fact, throughout his career Frazelle composed many of his musical scores first with sketches because that, he said, is "what my eye hears."

As part of his residency, he challenged his new young friends to *listen* to the painting for the next four weeks. Each day the children would walk down the street from their school to the mansion-turned-museum and up to the third floor where *Europa* hung. Frazelle would greet them. They'd settle into their task of sitting and staring. And Frazelle's questions would go something like this: What did the children hear when they looked at the wind whipping Europa's scarf? What sounds could they describe from the distant waves crashing on the beach? Or from the sailors and the people on the shore? And what noises would those pudgy creatures make? What emotions did the children feel or hear or listen to as they stared at *Europa*?

Some days, the artist asked the children to assume the roles of certain characters in the painting. What would those characters say to each other? What kind of a dialogue could be heard? What would their voices sound like? From that dialogue they put the words into music. And then the children used their voices and bodies to create an original melody and rhythm.

Weeks later, when they all decided that they'd created just the right score and felt ready to perform, the students invited parents, classmates, and other teachers to join them in front of the painting. They sang their songs. Frazelle played his music. Eventually, they collected their scripts and published them in the form of a libretto.

The girls and boys, of course, who before might have thought a big old room like that in a big old mansion would have been scary or stuffy or even boring, suddenly thought a masterpiece painting was "cool." But they also came away knowing that art could—and often does—involve and inspire all of a person's senses.

In other words, they learned just how much they needed their ears and eyes and bodies to make sense of the story in front of them.

Isabella Stewart Gardner, the woman after whom the museum was named, would have been thrilled. She was born into a wealthy family in New York City, and during her first trip to Europe in 1854 as a teenager, she was smitten by the beauty of art, a love that never faded. Six years later, she married Jack Gardner, the son of an elite Boston family, but her New York roots often alienated her from Boston's aristocracy. She struggled to fit in. She felt like an outsider. And as a result, she developed a keen empathy for those who might have felt marginalized, namely artists and the poor.

Only a few years after they were married, tragedy landed especially hard when the Gardner's only child died of pneumonia at age two. The two were heartbroken over their son's death. Though she was a devout Episcopalian, Mrs. Jack (as she became known throughout Boston) felt far from God and uncertain what she should do. Her husband suggested they sail to Europe, hoping the time away would help them grieve, and she agreed. What she couldn't have known—or expected—was just what else that trip might provide. She only knew her baby had died.

Something powerful did happen during their time away. She stared long and hard at one painting, and then another and another. The art she and her husband experienced throughout France and Italy absorbed them and inspired them, so much so that their grief slowly began to lose its grip. The paintings and sculptures and architecture in the churches and the buildings they visited began to soothe her soul, to draw her out of her despair. Each cathedral they walked into, each stained glass image she saw, helped her breathe a little more fully. So much so that Mrs. Jack's life changed on that trip at the same time as her passion and vocation became clear: she would spend her life promoting the beauty and inspiration of art. And she would do it by collecting dramatic paintings, religious sculptures, stained glass, and a variety of other works.

One of the first paintings Mrs. Jack purchased was Titian's *Europa*. Eventually, the couple's collection—2,500 works of art in all—outgrew their Boston Back Bay home, and they began plans to build a museum-like home that could also display their art for others. They invited an architect to design the new building, with courtyards for natural light and large rooms with high ceilings that would provide the space each work deserved. But tragedy struck again: Jack died before the plans were finalized. And again Isabella looked to colors and stones and sounds as a means of helping her heal.

She found a plot of land in Boston's Fenway area, purchased it, and oversaw the building of a museum that could display the many works she and her husband had collected. Each one had a memory, each a story as intimate as their marriage had been. In 1901 the building was complete, and she spent the year living in its fourth-floor apartment while she installed each piece of art herself—holding it carefully, positioning it just so, listening to the "sounds" it might make on the walls or in the light.

On January 1, 1903, Isabella Stewart Gardner opened her home and her museum to the people of Boston, inviting friends and strangers alike to a reception and performance by members of the Boston Symphony Orchestra, who played Bach, Mozart, and Schumann. From that point on, she insisted on providing space for artists, musicians, writers, and thinkers while allowing families from all economic backgrounds to tour her home and enjoy the plants and flowers of the courtyards, the galleries of Renaissance paintings, and the many rooms with crosses, stained glass, and statues. Often visitors heard violins or listened to lectures or smelled the flowers blooming in the courtyards. Always they were (and still are) greeted by a vision that had come from a generous love of art, one born in tragedy but built on the senses of a lifetime.

Around each corner, it wasn't hard to hear Mrs. Jack's passionate voice whispering what she had said not long after she opened her doors to her neighbors: "Years ago I decided that the greatest need in our Country was Art. . . . We were a very young country and had very few opportunities of seeing beautiful things, works of art. . . . So, I determined to make it my life's work if I could."[1]

Today, visitors experience much the same thing as they did that New Year's Day in 1903. In fact, the Isabella Stewart Gardner Museum has remained essentially unchanged. When Mrs. Jack died in 1924 at age eighty-four, not only did she continue her concern for the marginalized by leaving sizable financial gifts to the Massachusetts Society for the Prevention of Cruelty to Children, the Industrial School for Crippled and Deformed Children, and the Massachusetts Society for the Prevention of Cruelty to Animals, but she also established an endowment of one million dollars and specific stipulations for the ongoing support of her museum. Her will required that her permanent collection not be altered from how she had placed it with her own hands. After all, she had entertained a variety of artists and writers of her time—including John Singer Sargent, James McNeill Whistler, and Henry James—always believing that great art should inspire other artists. And she believed that the best art demanded all of a person's senses—her eyes, ears, and hands—to create the beauty she'd been given to share and to live well.

That tradition has continued ever since, which was why a group of fifth-grade children spent a month staring at a classic painting and creating music.

Sitting Together

True to its founder's vision, the Isabella Stewart Gardner Museum still inspires visitors who come from throughout the world. In many ways the mansion is the personal history of an extravagant and somewhat eccentric woman. But it is one that invites everyone who walks through its doors to participate in the history of art itself, all while creating new and vibrant responses with each visit or special event.

The museum also points to another reality, one that has inspired countless children and adults alike from across the centuries. *That* reality is a story that has remained at the center of Western art and become its very standard: the cross and resurrection of Jesus Christ. For on each floor in each room and wing of the Fenway mansion hangs a painted or sculpted testament to Jesus himself. After all, artists—regardless of religion—have been compelled through the ages to re-create the stories of Christ's ministry, death, and life, to translate the mystery and authenticity of his presence in history across their canvases or through their creative efforts. In art, Jesus has never been a mere idea.

Rather, his story—and all those that have pointed to him in biblical history—has remained at the center of Western art as the quintessential subject matter to study and to depict. Why? Because the story of Jesus Christ reveals a living, feeling person whose presence affected the world more than any other. And as a result, he has lingered long in the consciousness of many creative and gifted artists, most of whom have wrestled with all their own senses to understand and produce the images of his life on earth as honestly as they could. The works of their eyes and ears and hands have come together in each visual and creative representation of his life. The Gardner Museum bears testimony.

In many ways, such artists are both the proof and the fruit of those early followers of Christ who gathered together on that same day when Mary, the women, and Cleopas and his friend had seen with their own eyes (and heard with their own ears) the Lord himself. These disciples in the upper room were driven by emotion, desperate for inspiration, and keenly aware of their many needs—physical, emotional, and spiritual. They were grieving. They'd experienced a shared tragedy. And they didn't know what else to do but sit together in a drafty old room, staring at the drama of their pain.

The story that Luke and John both record of Christ's friends in a locked room is as rich with detail as the strokes on Titian's *Europa* and requires all of our senses to fully appreciate it. There they were: several from the inner circle plus family or friends, huddling together in a small space that was upstairs and away from common gathering places. Peter and John were likely there, though neither of the Gospel writers gives us a list of the names of those who were present. We do know, however, that Thomas was *not* there (though we'll explore his story in the next chapter) and that these men and women who were still together—in an apartment with dinner nearby—had been Christ's closest friends.

Nonetheless, they'd locked the doors. They were hiding from the Jewish authorities, I'm sure, from fear of persecution for having followed the rabbi who'd been murdered. After all, the disciples had been publicly connected to the "criminal" Jesus, so they would have been marked men and women, guilty by association. Locking the doors meant they did not want anyone to come in. It was their protection. Their fear had made them—as fear often does—irrational and desperate, keeping them from perceiving the situation as it really was.

But why had they stayed together? Was it terror, or was it friendship? Maybe both. Or was it a remnant of belief or courage from Christ's influence over the last three years that kept them together? Or maybe they'd stayed together because of the familiarity that comes when you've traveled many miles with one another, shared work and meals, sights and sounds, month after month for three years. Perhaps they just did not want to believe that *that* life together was over, really over.

Imagine the discussion and emotions that must have swirled around as they sat on the floor in that locked room. First they'd listened to some bizarre accounts from the women, then Mary, now from Cleopas and his companion, who were struggling to catch their breath having just run seven miles in the night. Peter and John had seen an empty tomb, so they knew that much had been true. Now Cleopas and his friend were beside themselves with emotion; they'd just chatted and eaten with Jesus. Really. He *was* alive, they exclaimed.

Heads shook. Eyebrows furrowed. Were the two sure they'd seen *him*? How did they know they'd not been hallucinating?

Did they really hear *his* voice and not someone else's? And if it was true, how could they possibly get their minds around this? Perhaps they were asking Cleopas to go over the details one more time, just in case he'd missed something. (I can imagine Mary and the women rolling their eyes, chuckling in confidence from knowing what the others did not.) Still, things were not exactly adding up. This account was simply too strange, too unbelievable.

No matter. They were so absorbed in the chatter that no one quite noticed when someone else was suddenly standing among them. While they were still bickering, checking the details and doubts and impossibilities of the stories they were hearing, Jesus himself appeared to them. Just appeared. As flesh and blood, in a room that was bolted shut. It doesn't really matter how he got there, just that he *was* there, standing among not a group of hysterical women, or a solitary grieving woman, or even two discouraged acquaintances heading home. He stood among all of those who comprised his inner circle of friends—and then some—as they gathered in a drafty old room, trying to make sense of what was now before them.

It was his first community appearance, and it had already been quite a day.

Emotional Collision

Imagine the frenzy of that moment (in Luke 24:37) when "they were startled and frightened, thinking they saw a ghost." This was how they responded even *after* Jesus had already said, "Peace be with you" (v. 36). For suddenly, out of nowhere, this unknown *being* was standing in front of them, not *exactly* one of them but in the shape and form of a man nonetheless.

No wonder they were frightened: it was dark, with barely a candle lit or a fire casting a shadow across the room. To suddenly see a figure appearing—like a stranger around a campfire—would have been terrifying indeed. And when they

101

did, someone probably screamed, another shrieked. What was it? Were they *all* seeing an apparition? A phantom? An otherworldly creature that had come to steal their souls? Or had a Roman officer somehow bullied his way in when they were talking and now come to drag them away to the same fate Jesus endured?

Elbows flew, eyes widened. They bumped into each other. Someone cowered in the corner; others grabbed each other and held on for dear life. More screamed. Someone probably fainted. But not one of them—not a single one of these ragtag friends of Jesus—had the wherewithal to fling open the locked door and run off.

They didn't have time. Just as they were fumbling into each other, shrieking and sweating and scared out of their minds, the image spoke again. This time his voice sounded familiar. They caught a quick breath. And the more they stared, the more they heard a sound they never would have imagined they'd be hearing at this time, in this place. It *was* Jesus, alive and in the flesh, talking to them and wondering what was the matter with them: "Why are you troubled, and why do doubts rise in your mind? Look at my hands and my feet. It is I myself! Touch me and see; a ghost does not have flesh and bones as you see I have" (vv. 38–39).

Someone relaxed his grip on another. Someone else, Peter probably, quit cowering in the corner and inched closer toward the voice. John probably brought over a lamp close to the man. And Mary Magdalene, Joanna, Mary the mother of James, Cleopas and his friend all stood up straight. They smiled. They raised their shoulders. See? They'd been right all along, and now the others were seeing *and* hearing him as well.

It is understandable that the disciples would have responded to Christ's appearance with fear. Nothing could have explained the appearance of a dead man now alive. It didn't make sense to their rational minds, and as a result, an immediate and intense intellectual conflict was battling with the physical reality of the moment. Their hearts were in tension with their heads, their eyes at war with their minds. They wanted to believe, but how could they? It was a moment when every reality they'd ever experienced was once again turned upside down and rearranged.

And so Jesus—the giver of life, the Word made flesh, the Son of Man—appealed to their senses. He didn't try to explain the physical dynamics of cosmic power over human beings. He didn't provide scientific evidence to support the theory of his appearance as both God and man when both seemed to have died three days before. He simply asked them a question about what they were seeing. It was a question like many he had asked them before: "Do you still not know me? Do you still not believe?"

Yet when he saw the terror on their faces, he invited them not to spiritualize the moment but to be human. How? By touching *his* humanity. He acknowledged their intellectual confusion and their emotional horror by redefining what they before had known as real. He asked them to touch, to listen, to look, and to see. And as they did, they realized: this was no phantom. This was no hallucination after all. Their friends had *not* been making up stories just to comfort themselves in their loss.

But the words he spoke were as intensely dramatic as his appearance. He reminded them of his death by pointing to his wounds—which they also had not fully understood. He was recalling for them what they would need to know from here on out, what would be the center of their purpose every day on earth: that he had indeed been crucified for their sake, and here were the marks to prove it, to prove what he had gone through to overcome their sin, to bring their fearful, flawed humanity into an eternal relationship with the perfect, loving Almighty who transcended every mortal reality they'd known.

This *was* Jesus, this *was* the one with whom they'd journeyed throughout Jerusalem, the one with whom they'd eaten and walked, and the one they'd been awestruck by as he walked across water, as he healed sick people and even brought three corpses back to life. This man, this image now in front of them, was no imaginary memory but was in fact the human leader they had followed on dusty roads for three years. And he was clearly also God as he had claimed, since now he was no longer dead.

In case they were tempted to believe otherwise, Jesus revealed to them the ultimate human trait, the one clue that was sure to seal the deal for them that he was alive as both man and God. He did this when he asked them one simple question: "Do you have anything here to eat?" (v. 41). And because they had just finished dinner themselves, they scurried over to the fire, grabbed a juicy piece of broiled fish, and saw the man from Galilee cut it up and pop it in his mouth. Then he swallowed it, "in their presence," Luke tells us (v. 43), so they could be sure they were not imagining things.

He ate in front of them, as all these frightened friends sitting in a locked room stared. And when he was finally finished, he returned the favor: he gave them food of another kind. Just as he had on the Emmaus road, Jesus offered his friends a nourishing course of biblical words; from Moses and the Prophets to the Psalms, he helped them see how each pointed to him, the Bread of Life, their unending sustenance.

"He opened their minds," Luke wrote (v. 45). As he did, the war within them ceased (or at least slowed), and they were no longer baffled. They understood. With all their eyes and ears and hands.

Group Lessons

It is not difficult to understand why the disciples were filled with joy and amazement when Jesus broke through their grief-filled room. Nor how their emotions suddenly overcame them, moving beyond their intellects and shooting truth straight into their hearts. Jesus peeled back their disbelief and took them beyond their intellectual or emotional responses, beyond the law of nature or rational thinking in the moment into something far bigger—faith. His physical presence helped them understand what their minds never would, because "faith is being sure of what we hope for and certain of what we do not see" (Heb. 11:1).

But because believing can be a long, slow process, he let them watch him eat before offering them the help he knew they'd need to anchor their faith. When he'd swallowed the last of the broiled fish, he began renewing their minds. How? With that which was already familiar but now fulfilled before their eyes: Scripture. They had been like children staring at a painting they didn't understand. They needed guidance as well as questions and wisdom larger than their own. In the midst of their chaos and fear, the hope of a living God invited them—as he still does—to participate in a celebration of all that he had created (humanity) and all that he had said (Scripture). He invited them to, in the words of Paul to his friend Timothy, "take hold of the life that is truly life" (1 Tim. 6:19).

What's more, he did so when the disciples were together—and I think this is a crucial point. Not only did he affirm their humanity by inviting them to touch his, but he appeared to them in community because he cared about their collective life together. It was his mission, reflected from his own being as part of the Holy Trinity. "As the Father has sent me, I am sending you," he said in John 20:21. And both John and Luke record Christ's direction to his friends to receive power from the Holy Spirit. In other words, he was reminding them that his community was theirs, that their life together was modeled after his and was only possible through the community of the Trinity: Father, Son, and Holy Spirit.

Though they'd been startled by his presence, doing exactly the opposite of what he'd said by choosing fear instead of peace, he nevertheless came to them in their frailties to build their faith and life together, despite their flaws. He called them to trust, as he does us, though they were prone to fear or worry as we are. He called them to forgive, as he does us, though they were tempted to demonize those who'd opposed them. He reminded them that his sacrificial commitment to them would be the center of their existence, though they, like us, had been quick to forget.

Each instance—as confirmed in both Gospel narratives—reminds us how we need the community of the body of Christ, the local church, in the same way we need the community of God the Father, Son, and Holy Spirit to help us respond as he asks. The disciples had merely gathered together in their fear and desperation, and yet there, in that place, Jesus restored their sense of hope and purpose and friendship. It was his presence alone—not any one thing or single deed they had done as individuals or friends—that reinvigorated and redirected them. If anything, they had failed in every way to believe or to serve. The only thing in their favor was that they were with one another. And Christ's message, if it had been about anything, had been about this: those who would follow him would be able to do so only when they gathered around his death and his life. Together. Staring hard at the man in front of them while sitting next to one another.

Community was a priority for Jesus, birthed out of his own community with God the Father and Holy Spirit and solidified through the price he paid on the cross. Together his disciples were merely children fidgeting on the floor in a drafty room. But together *with* his guidance and presence, they could hear and see and feel as he'd always hoped they would. The possibilities now of their life together—centered on their undying friendship with and submission to the Trinity—would be rich, generous, and extravagant.

Its ripple effect would be felt across the centuries.

Transformed Together

The disciples were changed because—and only because—Jesus opened their minds when they'd come together in the upper room. He did so through the powerful combination of Scripture, the presence of the Trinity, and the presence of each other. Why? So they could understand his purpose for them as a body of believers, not a bunch of individuals. He went on to tell them, to tell us, that they were now his witnesses to the reality of what they'd seen with their own eyes and to the message of repentance, forgiveness of sins, and new life. He was sending them out now as representatives of that resurrection story. He was confirming *his* life in them. He was giving direction and purpose, shapes and colors to them. And nothing would compare with their life together.

They "woke up" when he took a meal that harkened to another previous one—the Last Supper, when he offered their first communion, the Bread of Life, the sacrifice for their sins. They weren't changed when he'd appeared to Cleopas and his friend on the road or when they had gathered together in their collective despair in that locked room (though that probably got them ready). They were changed when he, the Resurrected One, personally reminded them of his broken body. By pursuing them—individually and together—he took the initiative as he always had to bring them hope, to restore their vision, and to set them apart with, and for, his purposes.

As Leslie Newbigin said in his book on John, *The Light Has Come*, "The empty tomb and the appearances to the disciples (in the upper room) are but signs to lead them to the new reality, which is an abiding in him as he forever abides in the Father through the presence of the Spirit."[2] They were to be sent as literal witnesses together of the forgiveness of sins, of a mission that would require they abide in the Father, remain sanctified in the truth of Christ and empowered through the Spirit they would receive together at Pentecost.

Their corporate witness of his resurrected life anchored their relationships with one another as well as their collective ministry; what they had seen and heard and touched literally sent them out into the world to point others to the source of their newly found peace. The grief they had felt from his death had been healed by the image now before them, and as a result they could not help but invite others into the safety and comfort of their life together, their eternal home, their heavenly mansion.

Likewise, we can be transformed from the daily despair of our sinful lives to the newness of abundant life by being in the presence of the Risen One and by regularly partaking of his sacrificial and broken life with others. It is in Holy Communion and in regular meals together, in consistent and corporate worship that we are formed and reminded again and again of the one who has always been who he said he was, the one to whom all of Scripture points and whose creativity spills over into us: the Maker and Messiah. The Prince of Peace, the Savior of the world. The Lamb of God. Our only hope.

That person is the one whose music can still be heard on the walls and windows of the creative lives around us if we're willing to stare long and hard, if we're willing to listen together.

——— In-between Reflection ———

1. What works of art—paintings, music, sculptures, the-atre, films, and so on—have particularly inspired you in your faith? Which have helped you understand something deeper about Jesus or life in community?
2. In what ways have you had to trust without evidence you could see with your eyes? How is faith a mystery that is hard to understand intellectually?
3. Why do you think Jesus appeared in flesh and bone to his disciples when he could have chosen any manifestation? What does his humanity say to you?
4. What does the Holy Trinity teach you about relationships? How can you and your friends keep from becoming dull to the resurrection?

5. What role could forgiveness play in unity? How might a lack of forgiveness taint community? In what ways do you need to forgive?

PRAYER:

Thank you, Holy Trinity, that you continue to inspire creative works in me and those around me. Lead me into fellowship with others centered on you so that those who don't yet know you might see you in our lives together. For your sake, amen.

—— PREPARATION ——

Please take a few moments right now to read John 20:24–31 printed below. It is John's account recorded in Scripture of Christ encountering Thomas a week after he appeared to the other disciples. Once you've read it, pause for a quiet moment to consider the words you've read.

JOHN 20:24–31

Now Thomas (called Didymus), one of the Twelve, was not with the disciples when Jesus came. So the other disciples told him, "We have seen the Lord!"

But he said to them, "Unless I see the nail marks in his hands and put my finger where the nails were, and put my hand into his side, I will not believe it."

A week later his disciples were in the house again, and Thomas was with them. Though the doors were locked, Jesus came and stood among them and said, "Peace be with you!" Then he said to Thomas, "Put your finger here; see my hands. Reach out your hand and put it into my side. Stop doubting and believe."

Thomas said to him, "My Lord and my God!"

Then Jesus told him, "Because you have seen me, you have believed; blessed are those who have not seen and yet have believed."

Jesus did many other miraculous signs in the presence of his disciples, which are not recorded in this book. But these are written that you may believe that Jesus is the Christ, the Son of God, and that by believing you may have life in his name.

When you are ready, continue reflecting on the following question:

Perhaps you've read this story before. What insights or observations did you notice as you read the story anew in John's account? Jot them down. Take a few moments to reflect before reading the next chapter.

PRAYER:

Dear Lord, your grace in the person of Jesus Christ is my help when I am tempted to doubt. Please help my unbelief. Amen.

6

Doubting Voices

When my husband and I were approaching our tenth wedding anniversary, we were in the middle of a cold New England January. It was also a challenging economic time, and we wondered how, or if, we would be able to do anything to celebrate. For weeks we talked about if we would take the time off of work, and if we could, if the weather would permit us to travel, even to a local restaurant for a nice meal. Blizzards had canceled a few dates already.

Then one day my husband surprised me with the news that we would be taking a short trip the weekend of our anniversary. He wouldn't tell me where we were going, just that we would be getting out of the winter for a few days to celebrate.

I confess, though, I had my doubts. I wanted to believe he'd be taking us on some extravagant—and warm—journey, but I knew the limits of our budget. When I pressed him, he would only smile. He did tell me I might need my swimming suit and comfortable walking shoes, maybe a light jacket.

Would I need suntan lotion? Probably not, he said. What about shorts or sandals? He shook his head, shrugged, and told me he wouldn't divulge any more information.

"Trust me," he said. "It'll be fun."

Even at the airport, I was skeptical. When we arrived at the gate, it was obvious that we were catching a connecting flight, so we could have been going anywhere. I stared at the people around us, and in spite of the reality of our bank account and the hints my husband had given me, I did what I think any American woman might: I began to fantasize. Maybe my husband had secretly inherited a few thousand dollars and wanted to spend it on a Caribbean cruise, where we'd sit on the deck and watch the sun set on the ocean. Or maybe he'd worked a part-time job I didn't know about so we could go to one of those all-inclusive resorts in Mexico or Jamaica you read about in the travel section of the Sunday newspaper, where the swimming pool has a bar in the middle and they serve you fruity drinks with miniature umbrellas. Or maybe he'd inherited *and* worked a secret job so that now we were going to a luxury spa on some exotic beach where we could get deep massages and body wraps and cucumber facials—a wild dream on my part since I wasn't sure my husband even knew what a spa was. But anything was possible . . . wasn't it?

I allowed myself to hope. I wanted to believe beyond our current financial situation and even felt slightly giddy about it once our plane took off. Then, when our plane landed in the city where we'd catch our connecting flight and we walked down the terminal, I saw the sign at the gate. I realized where we were going. Rather, I realized where we were *not* going. The reality of our budget slapped me from my reverie and I sighed loudly. I looked at my husband, who was not smiling. His eyes dropped. The last thing he wanted was for me to be disappointed or to question his judgment. But there it was: we were heading *not* to a beach resort or a fancy hotel or a cruise but to a small southern town on the coast where we would stay with one of my husband's closest friends. And his brother. In their bachelor pad house.

Not a swimming pool in sight.

Of course, once we arrived, it was fine. It *was* fun even. We explored the charming historic district of this town, walked along a river as the sun warmed our faces (not a snowflake in sight!), and rode bicycles past magnolias just starting to bloom. We caught up with our friends, ate fantastic local fish, and remembered a decade of trips and conversations. My husband and I even splurged one night at a gourmet restaurant and inn. No, it wasn't a cruise or a spa, but it was a perfect celebration of our life together. It was exactly what we needed.

Why, then, had I been disappointed when I first saw the name of the city where we were going? Why had I allowed my view of reality to grow into fantasyland? Why had I wanted to believe something else, no matter what my husband said?

It might be helpful to back up several years to our first year of marriage. Only a few months after our wedding, my husband brought out a series of books that he told me shaped his life and faith. Because the stories were profoundly influential, he wanted to share them with me. And so each night after work during our first year together, I'd lie on the couch and listen as he read out loud the wonderful and impossible adventures found in each of the seven books from C. S. Lewis's The Chronicles of Narnia.

I'm convinced now that the sheer act of reading a story aloud builds confidence in a relationship: children *believe* their parents when they read them stories, students *believe* their teachers when they turn the pages of a book, and wives *believe* their husbands when they share profound tales with them. Something magical happens in the transaction; something intimate and important and solidifying occurs when a human voice relays the drama and characters of a good story to the eager ears of another. Trust is built.

My husband was building—and reinforcing—our trust each time he read to me a tale from Narnia. And years later, as we enjoyed our anniversary trip in that southern town, celebrating a decade of memories and books and conversations, I found myself reflecting on that year I first heard him read The Chronicles of Narnia. Maybe it was because in the days before we left, I'd been listening to his voice describe the journey we were about to take, fueling my imagination to enter a world of possibilities and expectations, just as he had with those first Narnian adventures. And then maybe because I was feeling guilty that I had doubted him at all, I couldn't help but return to one scene in particular from one of Lewis's better-known tales. It seemed an obvious parallel.

In *The Lion, the Witch and the Wardrobe*, Lucy—an innocent little girl, you might remember—had selected a wardrobe as her spot during a game of hide-and-seek. But because it was not just any wardrobe, she slipped into the winter land of Narnia. There she met a caring faun and learned of an evil witch before somehow venturing back into the wardrobe and the house where her brothers and sister had been playing. When she tried to explain where she had been, they doubted she was telling the truth. How could she be?

Who falls into another world through a wardrobe in an old house?

But then her brother Edmund stumbled into Narnia too and became enchanted by the place—for all the wrong reasons. Still, Lucy took heart when he told her where he had been, until their older brother and sister challenged them. Edmund lied and told them they had only been *pretending* that Lucy's story about a country in the wardrobe was true. It was just for fun, he'd said. All nonsense.

Lucy's face dropped. The innocent little girl was crushed and ran from the room.

The older siblings, Peter and Susan, began to worry about their little sister. Ever since that first game of hide-and-seek and the silly tale about the wardrobe, they'd grown concerned. She had lost some of her sparkle. Though Edmund kept denying the wild accounts of winter and fauns, Lucy held to them as truth, no matter what her brothers and sister said.

I can still hear my husband's compassion as he read the lines, "It was not surprising that when they found Lucy, a good deal later, everyone could see she had been crying. Nothing they could say to her made any difference. She stuck to her story and said, 'I don't care what you think, and I don't care what you say. . . . I *know* I've met a Faun in there and I wish I'd stayed.'"[1]

The older children then felt compelled to get help. They went to their uncle, a professor, and explained to him how there must be something really wrong with Lucy. The professor listened carefully to Susan and Peter as they recounted the details of what had happened, until finally he cleared his throat and asked them the last thing they expected to hear: "How do you know that your sister's story is not true?"[2]

They were astonished, then even more so as he led them through a series of questions they had to consider in order to make sense of the situation: Who—Edmund or Lucy—was more reliable, more truthful? Lucy, of course, they said. Did they know how serious a charge it was to accuse someone whom they'd always found truthful of lying? Maybe she wasn't lying, he said. Surely they couldn't think Lucy was mad? They had only to talk with her and see her face to know she was not mad. Could there be another explanation?

The children were baffled that a grown-up could talk like this.

So the professor summarized for them the only three possibilities that explained the situation: "Either your sister is telling lies, or she is mad, or she is telling the truth. You know she doesn't tell lies and it is obvious that she is not mad. For the moment then and unless any further evidence turns up, we must assume that she is telling the truth." After all, he warned, "this is a very strange house." Anything was possible, so "there could be other worlds, all over the place, just round the corner."[3]

The children soon realized that Lucy had *not* been lying and they had no reason to doubt her. Her voice had been as trustworthy about Narnia as it had been about everything else she had ever told them. So they discovered their own inability to believe at the same time they discovered something they never expected: Narnia. The strange land *was* real. They even journeyed through its charming and dangerous woods and past rivers, houses, and creatures, making many new friends in the process and encountering an adventure far greater than anything they had ever experienced.

Lewis—himself a converted skeptic—spent the rest of the Chronicles exploring that other-world reality where nothing seemed impossible. And through his series of fantastic tales, Lewis showed us the incredible adventures that awaited children and adults alike when they listened to the voices of those closest to them and trusted them.

Meeting Another Skeptic

I'll always be grateful for our anniversary weekend away. Even if I did not understand it right away or wanted to believe something else, I knew my husband's judgment in planning our trip was reliable. Likewise, the themes and lessons found in The Chronicles of Narnia have reinforced my faith in Christ and trust in others, which is one reason they've secured their place on my list of favorite books. And because I'll always associate them with my husband's voice, they'll remain especially cherished stories. By reading them aloud to me, he began an early habit of exploring literary—and literal—lands with me. The more we've listened to each other's stories, the more our mutual trust has deepened.

But obviously, I still have my lapses. I'm still nagged by the fact that I questioned my husband during that anniversary trip in the same way Peter and Susan questioned Lucy. My expectations had grown into one thing, and something else materialized. Likewise, Peter and Susan had believed no one could hide in a wardrobe and end up in another land, until the unexpected happened: *they* themselves fell into Narnia!

The point is, it's not always easy learning to believe and not doubt the credible voices of those we love. It is a process often influenced by emotional baggage, cultural pressures, or intellectual conflicts. It can take years of daily personal interaction to appreciate the integrity of a friend, just as it requires a deep sense of grace to remain loyal to those family members or colleagues who might have caused us pain or disappointment. No matter how close or intimate two people have been, no matter how many memories or bonds have been created, the trust in human relationships can be quickly questioned, especially when something unbelievable is thrown into the mix.

And yet that single acknowledgment helps me appreciate all the more the story we now come to in John 20. Thomas is the one disciple who is best known not for what he believed or even what he did but for what he did *not* believe. It's difficult, in fact, to think of Thomas without also attaching the word *doubting* to his name.

But we can't be too hard on the guy, given how prone most of us (and I'm hoping I'm not alone here) are to skepticism and unbelief. Certainly there was more to Thomas than the infamous story of his doubt revealed in John's Gospel. Certainly he had his good qualities too.

The few details we're given in Scripture about Thomas before Christ's death reveal a glimpse of who he was as a person. A zealous, passionate man who sometimes used his nickname, Didymus, which in Greek meant *twin*, Thomas was listed with the names of Christ's twelve chosen followers; he was a part of the inner circle of the Lord. He probably was a fisherman, since he joined Peter and the others out in the boat for a night of fishing (see John 21), and he traveled with John, Matthew, and the others, including the women, during the three years Christ preached his good news. That meant he watched Christ do some spectacular deeds and heard some amazing sermons and prayers. Thomas seemed a loyal follower of Jesus, so much so that he was willing to step out and lead the other disciples in following their rabbi during a potentially dangerous time for him.

We know this about Thomas because of an interesting detail found in John 11. Jesus and his followers had been roaming the countryside for nearly three years already, creating many enemies in the process. In this chapter, Jesus was nearing the end of his ministry, escalating his status as a marked man by angering local authorities with his outrageous claims and miraculous healings. They were trying to seize him. Still, when Jesus was told that his friend Lazarus was dangerously sick and near death, he responded not by going to visit him but by staying put. For two days. Only then did he pick up his pack and tell his friends they were heading back to Judea.

Thomas was with him then; he heard his words, he listened to his voice. He trusted him.

Nonetheless, Thomas and the disciples warned Jesus of what would happen if he did go back; the Jews had already tried to stone him to death, so what worse fate might await him if he returned? Jesus went anyway, knowing two things: that by then Lazarus would be dead, wrapped in grave clothes, and buried, and that by calling forth the dead man from the grave, Jesus would absolutely usher in his own demise. Christ would raise Lazarus from the dead and win over many new believers—Thomas was a witness to the event—but in so doing, he would also incite the Jews and Pharisees, who began plotting his murder.

So when Jesus declared to his friends that he was returning to this volatile situation, Thomas, the loyalist, revealed his character in John 11:16: "Then Thomas (called Didymus) said to the rest of the disciples, 'Let us also go, that we may die with him.'" Or as Eugene Peterson put it in *The Message*, "That's when Thomas, the one called the Twin, said to his companions, 'Come along. We might as well die with him.'"

It was an extraordinary statement, hardly the stuff of a skeptic! What was it about Jesus that Thomas had come to love so much that he was willing to join him in his death, if it should come to that? Clearly, Thomas had recognized something essential about Jesus during the past three years. He had listened to enough stories while traveling throughout Judea that Thomas was not only willing to give up his own life for this man but also was willing to lead his other friends into a potentially horrific scenario. He showed courage here, not doubt.

Thomas—like the others—knew Jesus was in trouble. Less brave men would have abandoned Jesus entirely, afraid of what might await the Lord and afraid for their own lives because of their association with him. Others might have at least persuaded their friends to leave Jesus for their own safety. Instead, Thomas heard the determined voice of the young rabbi preparing to return to Judea, knowing who would be waiting for him and what might happen to him. Rather than doubting Christ's decision, Thomas rallied the troops to follow their leader. Not a shred of disbelief anywhere—only courage, devotion, and leadership.

But any soldier in the military or any supporter of a political candidate will tell you no matter how bad it looks, if you believe in your commander or your leader, you will expect him to prevail. And even if the odds are stacked against him, failure will not be an option. In the same way, I have to think that though Thomas knew the imminent danger that awaited Jesus, he would not have believed the Pharisees would defeat his master. No, I think he passionately expected Christ to become their Messiah, their king, their Savior. Thomas believed Jesus *would* be the one to usher in a new kingdom for Israel—alive and victorious.

All of which meant that Thomas did not anticipate the fate Jesus received, let alone endure what he did when he was stripped, flogged, and executed on a cross outside of town. Thomas had believed his leader would guide them; he did not expect Jesus would die.

Until he learned of the rabbi's corpse. And when he knew Jesus was dead, some flicker of faith must have died too.

Conflicting Messages

For three years, Thomas traveled with Jesus and their community of friends. He'd watched with them as Jesus walked across the top of the sea, when he'd straightened the spine of the crippled woman on the Sabbath, and when he'd called forth the dead man Lazarus from the tomb. Thomas had seen Jesus perform these and other miracles; he'd heard him tell his stories and parables; he'd listened to him preach of a coming kingdom; and he'd witnessed him challenge the religious and civil authorities. Together with the others, he'd shared daily life—meals, songs, laughter, journeys—with Christ. From such close, consistent interaction came an authentic trust in the rabbi.

When the guards dragged Jesus away to be whipped, tortured, and executed, Thomas was nearby. But he was caught in that tension that comes when you believe what is happening in front of you and yet you cannot believe intellectually that it could be happening. He was caught in that place where reality slammed into hope. It wasn't supposed to happen this way. He had expected Jesus to be different. How could he possibly die? How would Jesus save them, or bring in a new kingdom, if he were dead?

But Friday came, and Thomas was crushed. Disoriented. Despondent. Not only was Jesus no longer with him, but what he had believed about Jesus must not have been true. Then Saturday came—a long, unbearable day. Thomas probably hid with his friends, grieving, afraid, and dismayed now that Jesus was a corpse. He must have wondered what they'd do next, who they would be, where they'd go. Sure, he remembered Christ telling him, "I am the way and the truth and the life," when Thomas had been the one to ask him, "Lord, we don't know where you are going, so how can we know the way?" (John 14:5–6). But now there was no way and no truth. There was no life.

Thomas must have felt betrayed.

To add salt to his wound, by Sunday he'd listened to Mary and some of the women recount their fantastic tale of seeing the rabbi alive again. And then the unthinkable happened later that same night: *all* of his friends were agreeing with the women, claiming they too had seen the risen Jesus! Jesus, they told Thomas, had indeed entered their locked apartment on Sunday night; he'd even eaten a piece of broiled fish in their presence. But Thomas shook his head at the absurdity of it all. He didn't buy it. It couldn't be true.

I like how Frederick Buechner described it: "The disciples were hiding out in Jerusalem somewhere, scared out of their wits that the authorities who had taken care of Jesus would be arriving any moment to take care of them. They had bolted the door and were listening for the dreaded sound of footsteps on the stair when suddenly Jesus was among them. . . . They all heard what he said with their ears and saw how he looked with their eyes except Thomas."[4]

Where had Thomas been that night when his friends had gathered in that locked room, when they claimed to see a hungry, breathing Christ standing among them? Was he out getting food, visiting his family, or catching up on some sleep? Or was he keeping watch in case the Jews found them, trying to protect his friends?

John didn't give us the detail of where Thomas was that night, only the detail of where he was *not*. He was *not* in that upper room that day the Lord made his third appearance to his friends. He had not heard his voice or seen him eat or watched him stand among them. He had not looked with his own eyes on the man, though all of his closest friends in his life told him they had seen the Lord, that Mary and the women had been right after all.

Day after week after month, he had traveled with these same friends along countless dusty roads. They'd shared unbelievable experiences already, as well as mundane moments. They'd grown like a family. So why didn't he trust their account of the risen Lord? Why did he doubt such enthusiastic claims? Or in the logic of Lewis's professor, did he think they were lying to him? Were they mad or delusional? What made Thomas so determined not to trust their voices?

Could there have been another explanation?

Maybe it was the fact itself of Jesus's appearance—not the friends who claimed it—that was simply not believable. It was unprecedented. No one ever lived again who had died, just as no one ever entered a new land through a wardrobe. Jesus could not have been the king he'd said he would be if he could not even save himself on the cross. Disappointment had surely mixed in with despair for Thomas, a deadly combination that would always lead to doubt.

Still, I imagine Thomas probably wanted to believe his friends were right—he wanted the adventure they'd been on to continue. He wanted Jesus to be who he'd claimed to be. But his expectations had been trampled. The man he thought would save them had been crucified on a tree and then buried in a tomb. The pain of believing once and ending up betrayed had been hard enough. Maybe he convinced himself that he would not be made a fool twice. He would not believe again.

"He said to them, 'Unless I see the nail marks in his hands and put my finger where the nails were, and put my hand into his side, I will not believe it'" (John 20:25). No matter how many of their voices sounded credible, no matter how reasonable his friends seemed, Thomas knew this could not happen.

John tells us that an entire week passed after that interaction, and I suspect it must have been a very long week indeed for Thomas. Perhaps he listened to his friends' enthusiasm and stories over and over as they tried, like Lucy had, to convince him of what they'd seen. And he tried with resolute determination not to care what they said. How many of the disciples—

Peter, Matthew, James—would have tried to persuade their friend of the reality they *knew* they'd experienced? Surely they would have told Thomas day in and day out that they *knew* they'd seen the Lord, heard him, sat with him, watched him eat. And perhaps they would have felt hurt as well when Thomas did not believe them, each time he shook his head and said, "Not possible. No way. I won't believe unless I see it with my own eyes and touch him with my own hand."

Their words were not enough for him to believe the impossible. For him, hard evidence—physical proof—was more trustworthy than the voices he'd listened to for three years. He needed to experience Jesus for himself.

And to his astonishment, the Lord obliged.

The Lesson Arrived

Somehow, in what must have been a dismally long week of skepticism and challenges, fear and loneliness, Thomas managed to survive. After all, his friends were convinced of one thing, he another. But friends they remained nonetheless, so seven full days after the reports of those first appearances, Thomas still joined the others in that same room of that same apartment. They'd closed the doors again, locked them tight, still afraid of the Jews—if not more so since these absurd reports of sightings—and were probably about to pass the fish and chips when someone startled them with his presence. Once again in the middle of their fellowship, the Lord stood, returning for another visit to all of them, yes, but to one doubting soul in particular.

If Mary needed to hear her name spoken aloud from Jesus for her hope to be restored, or Cleopas needed to break bread with him, Thomas needed (or at least wanted) physical evidence to believe. Thankfully, Christ was not surprised or daunted by the demand; instead, he did what he always had during his ministry: he pursued even the most well-meaning and loyal skeptic where he was and as he was—with all his complexities and confusion and pride. Jesus sought out Thomas personally, tenderly, compassionately. He heard the quiet longing of Thomas's heart and smiled at his stubborn intellect.

First, though, Jesus challenged all their anxieties and questions with a simple pronouncement, "Peace be with you!" (John 20:26). They stood quietly, riveted by his voice. Then he looked around the room and found that one disciple who remained unconvinced, the one he had come for. Guiding the disciple as he spoke, Jesus said to Thomas: "Put your finger here; see my hands. Reach out your hand and put it into my side" (v. 27). Jesus didn't have to be so tender. He could simply have lectured Thomas, confirming his existence and chastising Thomas for his disbelief. Instead, in an exceedingly personal but gentle confrontation, he brought Thomas back into his inner circle, allowing Thomas to join the others who had already been restored by the truth of the one they loved—and had seen alive again!

In other words, Christ was inviting Thomas to touch the scars of his humanity, a touch that reminded Thomas and those watching of his death on the cross for their sakes. But he was also confirming for Thomas and the others the unprecedented reality of his power and life, that he had indeed risen victorious from the grave for their sake as well. Jesus was restoring that hope Thomas had once believed that Jesus *was* the Messiah, the Savior who would usher in God's kingdom. And as he held Thomas's hand in his side, he uttered a statement that only God in the flesh could make and only a God of love could extend as an invitation, one he makes to all of us: "Stop doubting and believe" (v. 27).

Thomas responded to Jesus's words and presence not with doubt but with recognition that Jesus was who he said he was all along: Lord and God. It was true! The others had not been lying or mad but *had* seen the risen Lord. It was Thomas who had been "mad" for questioning their judgment and their trustworthiness. Nonetheless, Christ transcended his intellectual conflicts and emotional despair by appearing personally to him as he gathered with the others, and in the process Jesus restored the trust within their community as well. In their fellowship together, Jesus singled out the skeptic, loved him, and reconciled him to the others.

He still does. Jesus still seeks out those of us, like Thomas, who live in a world of conflicting messages and personal battles, those who might need a unique touch or a specific answer. Undaunted by our demands for proof or our obstinate declarations, Jesus still goes to great lengths to find us and still visits us especially as we gather with our community of fellow believers and doubters. When he does, he still stands among us and says, "Peace be with you," breaking through the locked areas of our unbelief, the stubbornness of our individuality and self-assurance, and meets us with a grace far greater than all the doubts and cynicism and betrayal we've ever experienced combined.

He puts our hands where the nails were driven *for our sake* and invites us to believe.

Eye-Opening Change

God bless the Italian artist Caravaggio for giving us the incredible painting of this scene where doubt is changed into real faith, arrogance is transformed by grace, and Jesus is not at all intimidated by those who questioned his presence. In this seventeenth-century painting *Doubting Thomas*, sometimes called *The Incredulity of Saint Thomas*, Christ's shadowed and mysterious face is looking at Thomas's finger poking at the hole in his side while two disciples look on over his shoulder. Caravaggio's painting is shocking in its intimacy and beauty, yet when you stare at it, you can almost hear Thomas's words dropping like scales: "My Lord and my God" (John 20:28).

The image has not a shred of doubt anywhere in it. But your eye is drawn to one place only: the hole in Christ's side. That alone creates the personal and transformative faith.

And that is the most important part of Thomas's famous and true story. His skeptical heart was transformed not through the testimony of others, as trustworthy and credible as their voices might have been. He was not changed even when Christ first appeared in the midst of their gathering, as astounding as that surely was. But he was changed when Christ came to him personally, when Christ placed his holy hand on Thomas's and drew him in to the reality of an almighty love, a life that was truly life, a relationship that surpassed all others. Thomas changed when Christ encountered him at his most vulnerable place—his eyes—so that he could no longer doubt his existence. Christ alone initiated this new birth of faith; Christ alone guided Thomas into this new way of seeing. And because of this, nothing would be the same again for Thomas. He had witnessed something beyond what his own eyes beheld and his own hands touched. He had felt Christ's death with his own fingers and yet realized he was alive forevermore.

Jesus was *his* Lord and *his* God!

So what we ought to remember about Thomas is not his doubting and stubborn refusal to believe the testimony of his friends. What we ought to remember is what N. T. Wright calls "the greatest declaration of Christian faith in the whole gospel (20:28), the one clearly designed to remain in the reader's mind as the paradigm for all subsequent believing."[5] It was this personal recognition of the Lord that stoked the fire of his faith. And it was this declaration—*"My Lord and my God"*—that would move hundreds of thousands of believers long after Thomas poked his finger in Christ's flesh.

Still, Christ's final words to Thomas, "Blessed are those who have not seen and yet have believed" (John 20:29) echo loudly to us now more than ever. They challenge our modern-day thinking in an age of reason and scientific "evidence." In today's world, they can seem as silly and improbable as a cruise in January or a wardrobe into Narnia. As if that were not enough, John tells us that "Jesus did many other miraculous signs in the presence of his disciples, which are not recorded in this book. But these are written that you may believe that Jesus is the Christ, the Son of God, and that by believing you may have life in his name" (20:30–31).

In other words, the unprecedented claim of Jesus's life risen from the dead is strong enough to counter the relative thinking of our age, John writes. We're given just enough in his book—though Jesus unquestionably did more than we could imagine—to believe in Jesus's name and to receive the life that he offers. And by hearing such claims and stories, many professors and husbands, painters and skeptics through the years have been unable to dismiss them so easily. As Frederick Buechner put it:

> Nearly two thousand Easters have taken place since Thomas's day, two thousand years of people proclaiming that the tomb was empty and the dead Christ alive among men to heal, to sustain, to transform. But it is not enough. If we are to believe in his resurrection in a way that really matters, we must somehow see him for ourselves. And whatever we have so believed, it is because in some sense we have seen him. Now as then, it is not his absence from the empty tomb that convinces men but the shadow at least of his presence in their empty lives.[6]

Yes, we believe because Christ's "shadow" still falls on us through the mysterious work of his Holy Spirit, not because we see his broken body with our physical eyes. We believe because he builds our faith through the infinitely trustworthy message of his Holy Scriptures, not because we wonder about the sanity of believers around us. And we believe because he enlightens the eyes of our hearts through the prayers and communion of the saints as well as his incomparably great power in us, not because of anything we create on our own.

The more we listen, the more we will hear the voice of Jesus filling each room we enter with his peace. He will ignite our imaginations with holy expectations and create in us a trust that cannot be broken. So much so that we might even begin to wonder what would happen if we hid in a wardrobe or if surprisingly warm days were in store for us next winter.

— In-between Reflection —

1. Which part of Thomas's story can you most relate to right now? His zeal? His leadership? His doubt or his faith? Something else?

2. Have you ever expected something but been so disappointed that you didn't want to believe again? What happened? How did you grow from it?

3. What voices in your life—friends, family, colleagues, culture, self, or someone else's—most influence your decisions and shape your values? Which do you trust? Why?

4. Have you faced irreconcilable realities, such as the one Thomas faced? Is it difficult for you to believe in a man who died for your sins but lives forevermore? What does this mean for you in your daily devotions and routines?

5. Paul—another converted skeptic whose story we'll read later—wrote in Ephesians 1:18–21: "That power is like the working of his mighty strength, which he exerted in Christ when he raised him from the dead and seated him at his right hand in the heavenly realms, far above all rule and authority, power and dominion, and every title that can be given, not only in the present age but also in the one to come." How does this affect you now as a modern-day believer in Jesus?

PRAYER:

Thank you, Lord, that the evidence of your life and love resounds through history and yet is all around me and within me, through the power of your Holy Spirit. Help my unbelief today. Amen.

─── PREPARATION ───

Please take a few moments right now to read John 21:1–25, printed below. Jesus had appeared several times to all of the disciples, but this is John's specific account of Christ's personal interaction with and reinstatement of the apostle Peter. Once you've read it, pause for a quiet moment to consider the story you've just encountered.

JOHN 21:1–25

Afterward Jesus appeared again to his disciples, by the Sea of Tiberias. It happened this way: Simon Peter, Thomas (called Didymus), Nathanael from Cana in Galilee, the sons of Zebedee, and two other disciples were together. "I'm going out to fish," Simon Peter told them, and they said, "We'll go with you." So they went out and got into the boat, but that night they caught nothing.

Early in the morning, Jesus stood on the shore, but the disciples did not realize that it was Jesus.

He called out to them, "Friends, haven't you any fish?"

"No," they answered.

He said, "Throw your net on the right side of the boat and you will find some." When they did, they were unable to haul the net in because of the large number of fish.

Then the disciple whom Jesus loved said to Peter, "It is the Lord!" As soon as Simon Peter heard him say, "It is the Lord," he wrapped his outer garment around him (for he had taken it off) and jumped into the water. The other disciples followed in the boat, towing the net full of fish, for they were not far from shore, about a hundred yards. When they landed, they saw a fire of burning coals there with fish on it, and some bread.

Jesus said to them, "Bring some of the fish you have just caught."

Simon Peter climbed aboard and dragged the net ashore. It was full of large fish, 153, but even with so many the net was not torn. Jesus said to them, "Come and have breakfast." None of the disciples dared ask him, "Who are you?" They knew it was the Lord. Jesus came, took the bread and gave it to them, and did the same with the fish. This was now the third time Jesus appeared to his disciples after he was raised from the dead.

When they had finished eating, Jesus said to Simon Peter, "Simon son of John, do you truly love me more than these?"

"Yes, Lord," he said, "you know that I love you."

Jesus said, "Feed my lambs."

Again Jesus said, "Simon son of John, do you truly love me?"

He answered, "Yes, Lord, you know that I love you."

Jesus said, "Take care of my sheep."

The third time he said to him, "Simon son of John, do you love me?" Peter was hurt because Jesus asked him the third time, "Do you love me?" He said, "Lord, you know all things; you know that I love you."

Jesus said, "Feed my sheep. I tell you the truth, when you were younger you dressed yourself and went where you wanted; but when you are old you will stretch out your hands, and someone else will dress you and lead you where you do not want to go." Jesus said this to indicate the kind of death by which Peter would glorify God. Then he said to him, "Follow me!"

Peter turned and saw that the disciple whom Jesus loved was following them. (This was the one who had leaned back against Jesus at the supper and had said,

"Lord, who is going to betray you?") When Peter saw him, he asked, "Lord, what about him?"

Jesus answered, "If I want him to remain alive until I return, what is that to you? You must follow me." Because of this, the rumor spread among the brothers that this disciple would not die. But Jesus did not say that he would not die; he only said, "If I want him to remain alive until I return, what is that to you?"

This is the disciple who testifies to these things and who wrote them down. We know that his testimony is true.

Jesus did many other things as well. If every one of them were written down, I suppose that even the whole world would not have room for the books that would be written.

When you are ready, continue reflecting on the following question:

Perhaps you've read this story before. What insights or observations did you notice as you read the story anew in John's account of Peter's famous interaction? Jot them down. Take a few moments to reflect before reading the next chapter.

PRAYER:

Thank you, God of the universe, that you pursue us uniquely and ask us to love you because you first loved us. Help me today to love you by loving those around me. In Christ's name, amen.

7

Beach Fires

New York City was alive with ideas in the early 1920s. The First World War was just ending, the industrial revolution was transforming the economic landscape, and thousands of immigrants were seeking new opportunities in the Big Apple. In the whirlwind of such change, once-firm religious beliefs were also being challenged by intellectual and political ideologies. Young people like F. Scott Fitzgerald, Ernest Hemingway, and Eugene O'Neill were exchanging old ways of thinking for more "cosmopolitan" causes and forms of expression. It was the paradoxical era of Prohibition and women's rights, of vaudeville and Pentecostal revivals, of labor unions and extravagant lifestyles, and New York City was at the center of it all. If ever there was a precursor to the American culture wars of the 1980s and 1990s, New York's 1920s was it.

No wonder creative young people from all backgrounds gravitated there, hoping to do their part and claim their role in this new direction of the great democratic experiment. They wanted purpose and glamour. They worked for justice and meaning. They challenged Victorian and Protestant ethics in favor of personal indulgence and independence, which usually included lots of liquor, political protests, and sex.

New York City, in other words, was a magnet for anyone passionate about anything.

And so a young, blonde-haired woman with piercing eyes and a square jaw brought her ideals and skills to New York. She began writing about suffragist rallies for socialist newspapers. She wrote exposés about the dangerous working conditions in the factories on the Lower East Side of Manhattan. She poured herself into any cause that came her way. And she found herself visiting many a speakeasy (saloon), drinking alongside radicals like Malcolm Cowley and rising stars like O'Neill. She was a tough journalist with a soft spot for underdogs, justice, and men.

Love was never a smooth journey for her, nor easily defined. After a few failed attempts at relationships—which included an abortion and a divorce—the twentysomething-year-old reporter was determined to steer clear of the opposite sex and concentrate on her work. Radical friends tried to persuade her to go "Red" and join the Communist Party. Socialist editors continued sending her on confrontational assignments. And the creativity that exploded around the city in music halls, theaters, and clubs inspired her enough for her to try her own hand at novels and literary reviews. She was busy in her quest for meaning and mission; the only love she needed was the love of good whiskey, justice, and art.

What she hadn't counted on was the charm of a handsome North Carolinian biologist. Forster "Fred" Batterham, the brother of a close friend, was an anarchist and a gentleman with an agrarian sensibility. He intrigued the young reporter at the Greenwich Village cocktail party where they met, and she fell quickly, so much so that not long after, he convinced her to move in with him. Then with the same passion she had exerted while covering injustices and avoiding relationships, she dove into Fred's offer with a fervent "yes."

And so Dorothy Day became Batterham's lover and companion for almost five years, living with him in a beach cottage on Staten Island just across the harbor from Wall Street in lower Manhattan.

Dorothy kept busy with her writing, though she didn't stay in touch with as many of her radical friends. Fred seemed to be enough for her. In fact, the love Dorothy shared with him was enormously satisfying. They went for long walks beside the ocean and talked about the stories she was writing. They built fires on the beach and made romantic dinners by candlelight in their bungalow. The glow of fire had drawn her; something about the quiet dance of the flame pulled something deep from the woman's soul. And with Fred, it wasn't hard to be absorbed by his flame as well.

But it wasn't easy living with some of his convictions. He didn't believe in God or in marriage; both seemed absurd ideas to him considering how despairing the world already was. Besides, he and Dorothy didn't need the institution of religious traditions to affirm what they felt for each other. Though this saddened Dorothy, she contented herself with the invincible love they shared. She gave him all she had—her heart, her body, her days—because she was convinced they were together for a reason. She believed their love would sustain them.

Then Dorothy began to feel restless. Not because the passion in their relationship was dimming but because the opposite was true. She began to wonder how such an intense connection was humanly possible, how so much love could emerge out of two flawed humans. She considered the possibility that what they experienced might be a shadow of some other love, some other Being greater than either of them combined. And without saying much about it to her lover, Dorothy began to feel the pull of God's fire.

When she became pregnant, Fred hoped she would see the futility of bringing another human into an already troubled world. But Dorothy would not go down that path again. She hoped secretly that the baby might be the very thing that would draw Fred even closer to her, some deeper reason to reconsider a marriage together beyond his ideals against it. She even talked about it with a few of their neighbors, the nearest she had to friends on the island, Catholic nuns.

Fred didn't like the reality that a baby would disrupt their life together, and he liked even less the idea of Dorothy discussing their lives with religious women. Neither, however, kept Dorothy from visiting Mass at the only nearby church. She'd sit in the back of the church, eyes wide open, admiring the way others knelt at the altar, watching the flames of the votive candles dance while prayers were offered and Scriptures read.

Something—rather, Someone—drew her there.

A baby girl was born, and Fred, a decent Southern gentleman, did not turn his back on his partner or their daughter. He gave them bits and pieces of himself in those first months of the baby's life, helped Dorothy in caring for her, and held fast to his belief that nothing much was right in the world—except for a gorgeous daughter. The experience of birth for Dorothy, however, was profoundly spiritual and pivotal in her journey, one that she compared to the "beautiful rhythm of the sea . . . and when the nurse put her in my arms, I felt as if that which for so long had left the taste of hell in my mouth was being cleansed from my soul."[1]

Nonetheless, their baby's presence *was* a disruption to their devotion to one another, especially when Dorothy insisted on having their daughter baptized. Fred called the act nonsense, but he could not stop her. And during the ceremony of the baby's baptism, Dorothy herself was captivated. She was so moved by the beauty of the moment that she made a risky but certain decision: she would become baptized as well.

It was the risk of a lifetime, one she knew would drive a wedge between her and her lover. Even considering such a step toward a new kind of devotion sent her into an emotional chaos. She worried for days how he'd respond. She tried to talk about it with him, but he'd only shake his head in anger. Still, no matter how much she loved her man, she began to realize it was not enough for her soul.

Eventually her longing escalated, creating such a tension between them that Fred wondered what—or who—had managed to persuade an otherwise bright woman like Dorothy to consider this strange belief in religious faith. It nagged at him until finally he confronted her with the most painfully searching question of her life: how could she love anyone more than him? Who was the radical—or was he a madman—behind her decision?

His questions stunned her, so much so that all she could do was stare at him. As she did, she admitted to herself what she'd known for a while: he was suspicious of most beliefs and all religions. But she also realized something else: this time he was right. Someone *was* responsible for what she was feeling and what she wanted to do. As she put it in her autobiography, *The Long Loneliness*: "[He] knew there was no other man; but then I realized that there *was* another man, because God had become man and visited us and called each of us to Him, and so I said that to him; I said, 'It is Jesus, I guess it is Jesus Christ who is the one who is pushing me to the Catholics, because their church is His Church; He chose it.' [Fred] turned white as I had never seen him."[2]

While her radical friends were abandoning the religious heritage of the country, and her unbelieving partner was anguished with jealousy, Dorothy Day made a decision that would completely transform her life and countless others as a result. She'd come to this place of conversion not out of crisis but out of genuine love and happiness. Yet with a heart broken, she felt compelled to choose between two loves. It turned out to be the most difficult and liberating decision she would make, one that would move her into a mission among the urban poor that continues to this day. But it came at a painful personal cost, as she wrote:

> To become a Catholic meant for me to give up a mate with whom I was much in love. It got to the point where it was the simple question of whether I chose God or man. I chose God and I lost Forster. I was baptized on the Feast of The Holy Innocents, December 28, 1927. It was something I had to do. I was tired of following the devices and desires of my own heart, of doing what I wanted to do, what my desires told me to do, which always seemed to lead me astray. The cost was the loss of the man I loved, but it paid for the salvation of my child and myself.[3]

She'd come to the end of herself and realized God's love was the ultimate desire of her heart. He was what she longed for, even if it meant losing the life she'd shared with Fred. And it did.

When the stock market crashed two years later in 1929, ushering in the Great Depression and forcing thousands into poverty and homelessness, Dorothy Day responded with a new kind of passion. Her new devotion to Jesus prompted her to care for those around her. She provided meals and beds to the poor, and soon the Catholic Worker hospitality house and soup kitchen in New York's East Village neighborhood was born, not far from some of the socialist rallies she'd covered as a reporter. She went on to raise her daughter in the Catholic Worker community, and she spent her days in Christian service, always working toward justice. Her example inspired hundreds of others, and today Catholic Worker hospitality ministries remain important fixtures in many urban neighborhoods and farming communities across the United States.

No matter what she did or where she went until her death in 1980, Dorothy Day could not ignore the fire of God's Holy Spirit. He pulled her into a love far greater than the shadows she'd experienced before. And though she could not have known it when first she responded to his call, her decision would affect thousands of people for the next five decades in a work that continues to this day.

Another Beach Fire

I have been astounded by Dorothy Day's sacrificial decision ever since I first visited a Catholic Worker house in the urban neighborhood where I lived twenty years ago. Though Dorothy felt she'd failed many times in her relationships with men, Christ's grace and forgiveness drew her to himself in a way she didn't expect. She later wrote that sitting in that lonely pew in the small Staten Island church, watching others kneel and worship, sparked a longing in her to do the same, even if it meant alienating the man she loved. She couldn't help herself: Christ's love, she had come to realize, was like none other she'd known. And so in many ways, Jesus gave her the second chance she needed to live as she was created to: with a passionate devotion to him and his people.

Now at the intersection of one of the most beautiful stories in the Gospels—and one of my personal favorites—it isn't difficult to see an equally passionate and fiery soul in the person and disciple known as Simon Peter. A glance at the pages of his life with Christ gives us plenty of clues to understand his quick devotion, sharp mind, bold action, and intense feelings. Like Dorothy—and so many of us—Peter could be impulsive and yet vulnerable, tenderhearted and yet stubborn, reliable and yet unpredictable. He was quick to dive in to the cause and movement led by this new young carpenter from Galilee, no matter what it might cost him.

In fact, when Christ first called Peter to follow him (see Luke 5:1–11), Peter had been busy working as a tradesman, fishing with some buddies all night, and in much the same way as this account in John 21, they'd not caught a thing. Then—in both fishing stories—Jesus hollered out from the shore for them to cast their nets on the other side, though that first time Peter challenged him.

"Master," he called back to Jesus, "we've worked hard all night and haven't caught anything. But because you say so, I will let down the nets" (Luke 5:5). Both times, they pulled in the catch of the year. Both times, Peter left what would have made him a wealthy man to follow the man who gave him a deep sense of purpose.

" 'From now on you will catch men,' " Christ told him after that initial catch. "So they pulled their boats up on shore, left everything and followed him" (Luke 5:10–11). Something about Jesus drew Peter to leave all he had ever known or loved to follow someone he'd barely met.

And something about Jesus invited Peter over the next three years to feel as though he could say—or do—just about anything. It was Peter who dared to ask Jesus, in the middle of a storm, to allow him to get out of the boat he was in and walk on the water toward the Lord. It was Peter who, on the Mount of Transfiguration, told Jesus how good it was that he and two other disciples were there so they could build an altar for the Lord. And it was Peter who boldly proclaimed to Jesus that he would never leave him; even if all of the others abandoned him, Peter never would. He was convinced of his own unmoving love toward Jesus.

Of course, Peter was adept at speaking first, thinking later.

"A loose cannon," as one of my friends said of him, "and yet because we know so much about him (out of all the disciples) and his many imperfections, well, I can relate to him. Who isn't like him? Thank God for Peter."

Thank God indeed. So when we come to this particular interaction during Christ's forty days of resurrected appearances, we already know of Peter's resolute devotion. Yet we also know what happened to him once Jesus was arrested. Peter's loyalty quickly vanished, and he was thrown into an absolute crisis of faith for denying that he knew Jesus at all. Three times in the garden, Peter was asked if he knew Jesus, and three times he lied that he did not know the man; this, after devoting three years to living with the master, serving with him, watching him heal, listening to his sermons, and experiencing much grace for Peter's many, many blunders.

In the garden, Peter was no longer the cocky fisherman but a nervous coward who was afraid even to acknowledge any association with the teacher. And such a sense of failure sent him into a terrible despair.

It broke the passionate, devoted disciple and left him deeply wounded.[4]

Hard Confrontations

We come to this scene aware that Peter was despondent over his betrayal of the Lord, and even more so when he learned that Christ had been executed. In his mind, he believed he would never have an opportunity to right the wrong of those denials. Jesus was dead; how could he fix it? The pain of such regret must have been excruciating, a burden that would no doubt follow him everywhere he went. He had loved the Lord, yes, but that only made his ardent denial of their relationship all the more disappointing, all the more difficult to live with. In other words, he, like a young Dorothy Day, had followed the "devices and desires" of his own heart, and they once again seemed to lead him astray. Peter was crushed.

Three days later when he heard the women's shocking news of Christ's absence at the tomb, we should hardly be surprised to see Peter as the first to sprint toward the tomb, just in case it was true. Maybe he clung to a shred of hope for the opportunity to prove his love again to Jesus. Maybe the burden would be lifted. And even when he saw the Lord alive with their friends in the upper room, he must have hoped for a chance to address the mistake. But it didn't happen.

Though he and his friends had already seen the resurrected Lord with their own eyes and heard his challenges, according to John, Peter had gone back to what he knew best: fishing. Perhaps Peter was waiting for the commissioning Jesus had told them about and he was biding his time or raising some money to provide for his friends and family. We're not told why he returned to fishing, only that he did. And as both a vocational and spiritual leader, he easily persuaded Thomas and his buddies to join him.

But they had a bad night. They hadn't caught a single fish. No matter what they did, they'd been unable to catch a fish. As Leslie Newbigin described it in his book *The Light Has Come*, "Led by Peter, they have apparently turned their back on the traumatic events in Jerusalem to return to their old craft. But in this they meet total failure. A profitless night draws to its end, and they have yet to learn the truth of Jesus' words: 'Apart from me you can do nothing.' "[5]

On top of that, when they first heard Jesus call from the shore to cast their net on the other side, Peter and the others didn't recognize him. For all they knew, it was some stranger who had watched them from the shore, seen their empty nets, and called out to mock them. Or perhaps it was a guard from the local authorities waiting to report them as associates of that radical rabbi from Galilee. Out of all the people who could have been standing there on the beach, they didn't think it would be Jesus. And they didn't see that it was.

Why not? They'd seen the resurrected Christ already. Was the boat just far out enough from shore that they could hear his voice but not make out the figure? Maybe. Or perhaps his resurrected body—man but God—was just different enough that their eyes hadn't yet adjusted to the human miracle. Or perhaps they thought the couple of visits Jesus had made earlier were enough. Now they'd decided simply to return to the sea and wait for the final commissioning that Christ had promised.

Then they heard the voice again. And it *was* familiar, on many levels, even if they hadn't recognized him immediately. And that raises an interesting side question: what constituted recognition? Voice? Sight? Heart? Body? Or was recognition as unique to the person as Christ's ministry itself? Thomas said he needed to see and touch Jesus. Mary's eyes were opened when she heard Jesus say her name. Cleopas and his friend walked for hours with Jesus, listening to his voice, but it wasn't until they broke bread together that they recognized him. And like many believers since that first century, Dorothy Day was drawn to the rituals of worship when she first encountered Jesus.

How, then, would his followers recognize him from then on? How would they—would we—in the future? In the flesh? Through the Spirit? From the "sound" of his voice? As God, he could choose to reveal himself however he wanted to his followers. And so for those in relationship with the Holy Trinity, Jesus himself said, "My sheep will hear my voice and they will follow me" (see John 10:27).

His voice did not—and will not—change.

So perhaps when he called out to them again to cast their net on the other side and the haul was great, it finally registered in John's brain enough to connect the dots. "It is the Lord!" he exclaimed (John 21:7), and for Peter, the combination of the catch, Christ's voice, and now his friend John's proclamation must have triggered some realization of the truth that it was indeed the Lord there in the distance. An entire week after seeing the Lord twice already, Peter, the impulsive but passionate leader who had betrayed his Lord in the garden, now threw on his clothes—for it was not proper to approach a rabbi half naked—and dove into the water. He didn't wait for the boat to get to shore.

Maybe he wanted to reach Jesus before the others, to whisper some private apology, convey his remorse, and move quickly to the other tasks at hand. Instead, the dead-alive Man acted in such a way as to remind Peter—again—that he was not in charge. Jesus had his own agenda for the morning, and that included a "painfully searching question," as Newbigin called it,[6] with one of his more passionate and complicated followers.

It was a question of love.

Peter, breathing hard from his swim, made his way onto the sand about the same time his friends were tying up the ship. I imagine he was focused on the Lord, determined to fulfill his plan, no matter how chaotic the waves had been or how exhausted he was from fishing all night. By diving into the water and swimming to the Lord (a great example of his "act first, think later" approach to life), Peter made his devotion to the Lord clear . . . for the moment. And when Jesus said as he stood near the fire, "Bring some of the fish you have just caught," Peter was the disciple who jumped to and dragged from the boat the net teeming with fish (John 21:10–11). He was eager to please, to make right his errors, to express his love, but on his terms.

Obviously, though, Jesus didn't need a few extra fish to fry since he already had a pan going. The fact that he asked for some seemed both an act of genuine hospitality and a symbol of what he was about to do. Peter would be a fisher of men, remember? And Jesus would be Peter's provision at all times, no matter how often Peter might be tempted to think otherwise.

Certainly Jesus could have appeared to Peter and the others inside the boat, or he could have waited until they were back in the upper room. But he knew the beach was a significant place for their relationship; it was where he had first called Peter to follow him, and it was here again at the beach after a heavy catch of fish (153 to be exact) that he would restore Peter's heart. Despite all the ways Peter had failed Jesus, despite all Peter's impulsive acts and arrogant challenges and selfish deeds, despite even his betrayal in the garden and his painfully inconsistent devotion, Jesus loved him so much that he first cooked him breakfast. He loved Peter enough to ask him the most difficult questions of his life and then, amazingly, to offer him a second chance. And with that, an entirely new ministry.

Three times the fisherman had denied knowing the Christ; now three times Jesus gave him an opportunity to reconsider his answer, to re-create it or backpedal, if you will. "Simon son of John," Jesus said to him, referring to him by the name he used when they first met, a reminder to Peter that his sins had not changed Christ's identification of him as the rock on whom he would build his church. This dead-alive Man had secured the fisherman's identity and purpose by going to the cross and conquering the grave.

Then the Lord took the conversation in an intensely personal direction. Jesus asked Peter if he loved him. Here, the Greek word for love was *agape*, which is the highest and godliest form of love. And Peter, humbled and broken, responded by using the Greek word *phileo*, a word for love used mostly between friends. "Yes, Lord, you know that I am your friend," Peter said. Gone was the Peter who bragged to Jesus about never falling away from him. Gone was the Peter who boasted about going to his death for the Lord.

Again the Lord asked him about agape love, and again Peter responded with phileo friendship. But the third time, Jesus used phileo in his question. He asked Peter, "Are you my friend?" It was as if he wanted the disciple first to profess his love honestly and sincerely for his maker, establishing that as the place from which he would receive his "reinstatement" in the greatest movement Peter had ever known.

With Peter's love focused anew on his Lord, Jesus then charged Peter to abandon all thoughts of his former life and become a shepherd, inspiring not only an identity change but a new purpose. "Feed my lambs, care for my sheep," the Lord urged. Christ the Good Shepherd who laid down his life for the sheep was now redirecting one of his more stubborn creatures and in so doing imparting to him the same grace and ministry.

Peter, however, could not stop being Peter, even amid the excitement of their restored relationship as well as this new revelation of purpose. In typical "speak first, think later" fashion, his ears still ringing from the urgency of Christ's mission for him, he pointed to John and became distracted.

"What about him?" he asked Jesus (John 21:21). I want to imagine at this point the Lord grabbed Peter's chin, pulled it back before his face, and stared hard into those passionate eyes in front of him. Then he said, in astonishingly persistent love, "Never mind about anyone else. Follow me."

And though he could not have known it at the time, Peter's decision to follow Jesus would affect millions of people for centuries to come.

God built his church on it.

153 Visual Aids

The fire of Christ's love and grace drew Peter out of his emotional chaos and into the place of peace. Though Peter had denied knowing Jesus, it was Jesus who still called to him. Though Peter had tried hard to impress the Lord with deeds, it was Jesus who served *him* with breakfast. Though Peter was anxious to prove his devotion, it was Jesus who talked about love. And he did it not with criticism and rebuke but with painfully searching questions, questions that called Peter to choose his love.

Perhaps Jesus was there on the beach to remind Peter (again) that he did not—and would not—provide for himself. That was God's job. It was as if the 153 fish, as well as those Jesus had already thrown on the fire waiting for them when they came in from the boat, were reminders of the Lord's ongoing provision. It was a real catch of fish, surely, but they were also symbols for Peter—and for us—that despite our best efforts or deepest wounds, despite our grand plans or most painful decisions, Christ alone fulfills the longings of our hearts. No vocation, no beach house cottage, no other lover can give us what he can: love eternal.

The major event of this passage was not the fish fry, though the fish were certainly impressive object lessons of God's ability to provide above and beyond all that we ask or imagine, to use Paul's words. Instead, the marvelous scene of Peter's recommissioning on the beach was a reaffirmation of relationship. Not for Jesus, because his ministry to and compassion for Peter had not changed. But for Peter, whose faith and failure had indeed been tried in the fire of the Savior's love. As the 153 fish were an expression of God's ongoing care, Christ's three questions were an expression of his healing love. How? They offered Peter a second chance to explore his own heart, as if Peter had to hear himself determine his love for the one whose grace he could not ignore.

I love how N. T. Wright puts it in his book on hope:

> Now, with Easter, Peter is called to live in a new and different world. Where Thomas is called to a new kind of faith and Paul to a radically renewed hope, Peter is called to a new kind of love . . . "Simon, son of John," says Jesus, "do you love me?" There is a whole world in that question, a world of personal invitation and challenge, of the remaking of a human being after disloyalty and disaster, of the refashioning of epistemology to the new ontology, the question of what reality consists of.[7]

Yes, Peter would enter a whole new world through Christ's searching question by declaring his resurrected devotion to Jesus. In the same way, he asks us how much we love him, but not as a means to right some wrong or atone for some failure. He asks us for our love because he has first loved us. In the process of such a lifelong exchange, we experience the gift of restoration, direction, and worship. Each becomes a vital component for us to live with, and as a result of, the resurrected Jesus.

Nothing will delight the longings of our heart like the crucified and risen Jesus. Just as Dorothy Day discovered—in the same way Peter did—that the heart's ultimate desire is found only in Christ the risen Lord, so too can we feel the pull of his call toward him. Every romance or lover, vocation or status might be fulfilling for a time, but they are mere shadows of a fulfillment far greater than all combined. And every failure or shortcoming, betrayal or burden we've experienced can't begin to keep the Savior from loving us.

The cross already forgot them. The empty tomb confirmed the relationship.

Converted for a Purpose

The combination of the miraculous fish catch, Christ's generous act of hospitality, and his deeply personal conversation with Peter all fanned the flame of change in Peter's life. As a result of each, he declared his love to Jesus humbly and remorsefully and in direct response to the reality he experienced from Christ's love for him. Only out of first receiving God's love was he able to offer back his own.

In the same way, provision, hospitality, and conversation—like that which we see here between Jesus and Peter—are the flames that spark the fire of any conversion. They are the same flames that pulled Dorothy Day from a happy but wanting relationship to a far deeper and eternal one with the Prince of Peace, one that inspired her to reflect Christ's hospitality to the urban poor.

We know from other passages in the book of Acts and from history that Peter's life was radically changed by this encounter with Jesus on the beach. And we know that just as Christ told him, a life devoted to Christ would be costly, because Christ's love for us was costly. Peter's life would be an ongoing sacrifice for the kingdom, and it would not end gracefully: "I tell you the truth, when you were younger you dressed yourself and went where you wanted; but when you are old you will stretch out your hands, and someone else will dress you and lead you where you do not want to go" (John 21:18).

Three decades after his interactions with the resurrected Jesus, Peter was martyred in Rome under the emperor Nero. For Peter, loving Jesus meant offering his entire life for the sake of a truth and a love far greater than any other. It meant living a sacrificial and radical life as a result of that personal love, a life in which he went on to preach constantly, basing every message he proclaimed on the resurrection of his Lord.

He ministered to the poor, cared for the homeless, led his community, sent missionaries throughout the lands, and proclaimed the Good News of forgiveness to those in desperate need of it, even at the expense of his own comfort.

How could Peter go on to do so? Because he himself had been forgiven. Restored. Loved. Brought back from his lonely and shameful place of denial and redirected for an entirely new work. Peter became a new man, his passion secured in the passion of Christ. He entered an entirely new reality defined by the resurrection itself.

And the invitation for us is the same as it was for Peter, and for that matter Dorothy Day: to come to the end of ourselves, realizing our hearts' longing can be satisfied only with Jesus. When Peter listened to Christ's searching question, he did not get defensive or self-protective, recounting all the sacrifices he'd made for Jesus—that is, giving up his profitable fishing business, his home, and life as he'd known it. He couldn't say this because he knew all the deeds in the world hadn't proven his love. In fact, he'd failed in deed and would fail Jesus again. But Peter clearly heard the Lord inviting and affirming him in the greatest and only response we too can offer: love.

Yet Christ's gift of conversion came not through a rhetorical exercise or a spiritual love fest. It was through a deeply personal conversation with hard questions, during which Peter's soul was anchored in Christ's love, and in the same breath, he was given a monumental privilege to look outside of himself in service to others: *if* he loved Jesus, he would take care of his sheep. *If* he loved Jesus, he would feed his lambs. If we love Jesus, we too will feed others while we can. Mission was—and is—implicit in this love.

And so Jesus asked Peter—as he asked Dorothy and you and me—if he loved him more than these, more than any other aspect of life? More than your lover, your family, your career, your ministry? Or more than any other person who loves him? Jesus wasn't looking for a competitive response, as if Peter could win. Nor was he asking of Peter something

149

he could not humanly provide. But he was reminding Peter that the most fulfilling relationship he would ever experience would be with the man who had gone to the cross for him and then risen from the dead . . . so that he could have this conversation on the beach. And so that Peter could have a thousand other conversations from that point forward.

Christ's question to him echoes through the ages to the very place where we stand today: do you love me more than these?

It is a choice that will never disappoint.

── IN-BETWEEN REFLECTION ──

1. Dorothy Day was drawn to worship Jesus Christ, aware that his love was like no other she'd ever known. What part of her story resonates with you? How do you choose love?

2. Like he'd done with Dorothy, Christ dealt with Simon Peter in a way that seemed to parallel Peter's personal disappointments, specifically his denial of faith in the garden the night Christ was arrested. Here Jesus offers him three opportunities to profess his new love and faith. In what ways has God uniquely responded to you and led you in a new direction?

3. What was it about Jesus that motivated Peter to jump ship? What had happened to the disciple that made him so driven to see the man he'd so disappointed?

4. Review Luke 5:1–11. What is the difference between this fish catch in John 21 and the first? How is Peter's response different from the first catch? What might this suggest to you about God's provision of grace and love?

5. How does the idea of having breakfast on the beach with Jesus sound to you? What does it look like for you? In what ways is God asking you to revel in his love and forgiveness so that you might offer both to others?

Consider offering sacrificial hospitality to someone in your life who might not be expecting it as an expression of God's love for you.

PRAYER:

Gracious God, you call us to yourself so that we might be sent into the world. Help us to hear your voice today as we serve others in need. Amen.

PREPARATION

Please take a few moments right now to read Acts 1:1–14, printed below. Jesus had appeared several times to all of the disciples, but this is Luke's specific account of the ascension of Christ and the commissioning of the disciples. Once you've read it, pause for a quiet moment to consider the words you've read.

ACTS 1:1–14

In my former book, Theophilus, I wrote about all that Jesus began to do and to teach until the day he was taken up to heaven, after giving instructions through the Holy Spirit to the apostles he had chosen. After his suffering, he showed himself to these men and gave many convincing proofs that he was alive. He appeared to them over a period of forty days and spoke about the kingdom of God. On one occasion, while he was eating with them, he gave them this command: "Do not leave Jerusalem, but wait for the gift my Father promised, which you have heard me speak about. For John baptized with water, but in a few days you will be baptized with the Holy Spirit."

So when they met together, they asked him, "Lord, are you at this time going to restore the kingdom to Israel?"

He said to them: "It is not for you to know the times or dates the Father has set by his own authority. But you

151

will receive power when the Holy Spirit comes on you; and you will be my witnesses in Jerusalem, and in all Judea and Samaria, and to the ends of the earth."

After he said this, he was taken up before their very eyes, and a cloud hid him from their sight.

They were looking intently up into the sky as he was going, when suddenly two men dressed in white stood beside them. "Men of Galilee," they said, "why do you stand here looking into the sky? This same Jesus, who has been taken from you into heaven, will come back in the same way you have seen him go into heaven."

Then they returned to Jerusalem from the hill called the Mount of Olives, a Sabbath day's walk from the city. When they arrived, they went upstairs to the room where they were staying. Those present were Peter, John, James and Andrew; Philip and Thomas, Bartholomew and Matthew; James son of Alphaeus and Simon the Zealot, and Judas son of James. They all joined together constantly in prayer, along with the women and Mary the mother of Jesus, and with his brothers.

When you are ready, continue reflecting on the following question:

Perhaps you've read this story before. What insights or observations did you notice as you read of this great summary to Christ's forty days on earth after his death? Jot them down. Take a few moments to reflect before reading the next chapter.

PRAYER:

Father, Son, and Holy Spirit, thank you for your community of love, the same community that shapes us and sends us into the world as your ambassadors of reconciliation. Please instill in your church a deep sense of grace, peace, and forgiveness so that we might be witnesses of your living presence and love, now and always. Amen.

8

Sent Again

A few days before Christmas in 1941, families across England turned on their radios. Pearl Harbor had been bombed just weeks before, causing the United States and Britain to declare war on Japan. The year before, massive German air raids had descended on London, Southampton, Bristol, Liverpool, and Manchester, England, with no signs of letting up. Hitler's troops had already destroyed countless Jewish families, invaded Poland and Austria, and forced the people of Czechoslovakia, Greece, and Yugoslavia to surrender. Thousands of British, American, and Allied soldiers had already been killed fighting his evil, and only seven days after Pearl Harbor, Germany declared war on the United States. By December 19, 1941, Hitler had seized absolute control of the German army and launched one of the most far-reaching and horrific attacks ever to be unleashed in human history.

But on December 21, 1941, families and neighbors in England gathered around their brown upright radios not to listen to the latest updates on the unbelievable tragedy at hand. The newspapers and their own experiences had already provided them with plenty of despairing news about the war. Instead, they switched on their radios in flats and homes across the country and huddled in close to hear a dramatic program being aired by the British Broadcasting Corporation (BBC). It was the story of a particular baby in Bethlehem. He had been born outside a "shepherd's cottage," and his birth was celebrated by wise men with cockney accents but threatened by the Hitler of his time, King Herod.

From that first December night until October of the next year, the BBC aired eleven more of these radio plays about the life of Jesus Christ, written in modern dialect and delivered by a cast of talented English radio actors. Two years before, the BBC had commissioned Dorothy L. Sayers, a mystery writer turned dramatist and essayist, to write the series of plays on "the life of our Lord" for broadcasting during the Sunday *Children's Hour* program. The director of religious broadcasting for the BBC, J. W. Welch, felt such radio dramas were necessary because as he wrote in the introduction to the published play, the "dimension we call 'God' had largely vanished from their (listeners') lives; God was no longer a factor to be reckoned with in making decisions and the language of religion had lost most; everywhere was a great ignorance of Christian Faith. For example, of a group of men entering the Army only 23 percent knew the meaning of Easter. . . . Many had discovered it was possible and easy to live without any vital belief in God. He did not count."[1]

Though Welch was convinced of the plays' importance during those difficult times, he wondered how—and if—the series could, "for man today and in the language of today, make Christ and his story live again."[2]

Sayers agreed to try. She would write the plays on the condition that she could "introduce the character of Our Lord," use the same kind of realism she had in her other works, and deliver it in modern speech so that all could understand it.[3]

Welch was ecstatic. He found her conditions exactly as he had hoped, and *The Man Born to Be King* was broadcast in every town throughout England, repeated again the following year during the Lenten season.

As a result, thousands who rarely ventured into the Church of England as well as thousands of others who were weary or discouraged in their faith tuned in to the stories of Jesus as he walked the earth, healed the sick, and took on their sins at the cross. They cheered at his miracles and victories and wept over his arrest and gruesome execution. Soon they began to see this man—born nearly two thousand years before—as alive in a way that childhood experiences or stained glass images had never produced.

Two million people listened to Sayers's brilliant drama against the backdrop of wartime raids and food rations. And they responded with hundreds of letters to the BBC. Many admitted that *The Man Born to Be King* had shocked them, challenged them, and changed everything they'd ever known about Jesus. One man wrote, "I have been brought up to be a God-fearing man, and when a boy attended church five times every Sunday, but I will truthfully state that I learnt more about my religion in half an hour today than I ever did in the years of Sunday School." Another wrote, "Your play is quite changing the atmosphere in our house, and where there has been resentment and criticism, we can feel it dying away in the presence of Christ. I am sure this must be the case in all homes when they have heard it broadcast."[4]

Again, Welch was satisfied. His goal had been fulfilled, and the risk his corporation had taken to commission and produce the plays proved worth the effort. In fact, the last sentences of his introduction to the plays reflect his gratitude: "Miss Sayers has put the Christian Church in this country in their debt by making Our Lord—in her fine phrase—'really real' for so many of us. She has made a major contribution to the Church's essential task of revealing Christ. She has also, in my judgment, forced many of us to the grim task of considering afresh the awe-ful implications of the two words *incarnates est* (the Incarnation is)."[5]

For factory workers and businessmen to vicars, soldiers, and schoolteachers, all collectively enduring the horrors of World War II, Sayers's on-air proclamation of Christ's ministry, death, and resurrection renewed a country's hope. Through her radio plays, it was as if she'd been "sent" with the gospel message, one that helped countless women and men, boys and girls know that Jesus was indeed alive.

No wonder the title of the twelfth and final play in the series—about his resurrection—was called, "The King Comes to His Own."

The Sending

Sayers hadn't grown up expecting to write radio plays about Jesus that would reach her nation. But she had been raised the daughter of an Anglican vicar and had maintained a lifelong faith in the risen Lord, one she knew was relevant to all people in any time period. Christ was "really real" to her. This was why she excelled in her craft as a writer; she believed writing was her calling, and she was a careful and creative wordsmith. An amazingly gifted woman with a mind comparable to one of England's best-known apologists at the time, C. S. Lewis (in fact, she sometimes confronted Lewis on some of his theology), Sayers never lost sight of the reason behind her life and work: God's love expressed in the incarnation of Jesus Christ. The Word made flesh. Crucified and then risen. God with us.

But make no mistake: Sayers did not come to her faith in Christ on her own abilities or out of her own intellectual perspectives. Nor did Lewis or Welch or any of the other faithful Christians whose lives we've explored in this book. Just as those listening to *The Man Born to Be King* heard the story anew for themselves, each of these—as with each of us—learned about the grace of the Lord offered through his death on the cross *because of* the words and life of another human being. Each was then nurtured in his faith also through other Christians, usually in a local community called church where they gathered around Scripture, prayer, and song in worship. These believers themselves had mentors, who in the same way had been told and nurtured and encouraged in their faith by others, because those who had gone before them had experienced the same from others as well. Their corporate lives and shared history paid tribute to the work of the Holy Spirit, who has presided in and guided millions of women and men across the ages and continents as they have followed the living person of Jesus Christ.

There's a reason it's called Good News.

In other words, we are indeed surrounded by "a great cloud of witnesses," as the author of the book of Hebrews wrote (12:1). Many, many witnesses throughout history have encountered the "really real" life of Christ, one that started in that early church in the story we come to now in Acts 1, thanks to Luke the doctor and Gospel writer. He too was a faithful writer of "all that Jesus began to do and to teach until the day he was taken up to heaven" (Acts 1:1–2). And like Sayers's plays, Luke's summary here of Christ's life and ministry helped "listeners" hear the narrative of his time on earth with new ears: "After his suffering, he showed himself to these men and gave many convincing proofs that he was alive. He appeared to them over a period of forty days and spoke about the kingdom of God" (v. 3).

Not only did the proofs convince the disciples and those other first eyewitnesses of his reality, but Christ's words about God's kingdom inspired their mission together, creating a movement unparalleled to any in history, one that Luke recorded in the next twenty-eight chapters of Acts. But that movement, ironically, started first with something most westerners don't like: waiting.

Just as we read in each of the Gospel accounts, the risen Jesus told his followers here in Acts 1, "Do not leave Jerusalem, but wait for the gift my Father promised, which you have heard me speak about. For John baptized with water, but in a few days you will be baptized with the Holy Spirit" (vv. 4–5). Matthew wrote of the disciples going to Galilee, to the place where Jesus had told them to go before they could receive what many Christians refer to as the Great Commission. John began the commissioning narrative in chapter 20 in the upper room when Jesus breathed on them, whereas Mark conveyed a general overview of Christ's sending out of his disciples. And at the end of his Gospel, Luke described the beginning of Christ's commissioning and ascension but repeated it more specifically here in Acts.

Each narrative, though, points to that waiting period, that time between Christ's final appearance as a man in his ascension and that moment when God's Holy Spirit descended on them. It's important to note that the disciples did not get ahead of themselves. Though Peter knew of the mandate the Lord had given them to "be my witnesses in Jerusalem, and in all Judea and Samaria, and to the ends of the earth" (Acts 1:8), for once he restrained his passion and waited with the others as Christ had instructed. Thomas didn't rally the troops to go into battle, and Mary and the others didn't run and tell everyone they knew about the risen Lord. No, they did what they were told and waited for the fulfillment of his presence in their lives before they took another step. Yes, Jesus had said he'd be sending them into all the world to preach to all the nations, but they didn't move an inch until first they sat, together, in his temple, worshiping him and receiving the power of his Spirit. Then and only then would they be able to go.

Maybe these waiting periods were to remind them of the consistent truth they'd witnessed during Christ's ministry, during his death, and during the forty days he spent with them alive. It was the same message, after all, they'd learned in their own Jewish history: how God had always been communicating from the start of his story in Genesis, throughout the Old

Testament, and of course across the pages of the entire New Testament story. It was the same message Jesus himself unpacked first for Cleopas and his companion on the Emmaus road and later in the upper room with the other disciples. That message to his people was simply this: I AM. I am your hope. I am eternal truth. I am your God and you are my people.

Now, of course, the message had not changed, but the story of it had been fulfilled quite literally before their eyes. So when those early disciples saw and ate with and listened to the resurrected Jesus, when they waited for his Holy Spirit as he instructed them to do, and when they received his breath of life in them, everything they had ever heard him say or learned about their Messiah from their Jewish culture had come true. Their sense of purpose was now solidified, their eternal place with him secured. They no longer had a reason to be desperate for anything but him.

Armed with this new sense of hope from watching his sacrifice on the cross and then his resurrection from death, they would be able to encounter whatever might come their way to accomplish whatever he had given them to do. And as we know from the next chapters in Acts, they did wait for the promised Holy Spirit. And then they did go into all the world as a result. That ragtag, wishy-washy group of emotionally charged followers of Jesus, whose collective heart had been shattered when he died, formed the early church we see here in Acts 1. Together they watched as Jesus pulled the pieces of their brokenness back to a place of healing and love, as he always had before, and together they were empowered now by his Holy Spirit and sent now to do for others what he had done for them: console with his grace, confirm his promises, and commission others to do the same. The power of such love moved those first Christians through one town and the next and eventually throughout a good portion of the world with his message of peace and the truth of his presence.

They became his new body, still broken but alive. They became his new hands, still hurting but able to serve. They became his new voice, still ordinary but speaking Good News nonetheless. They'd been his eyewitnesses, and so they went. What might such a commissioning have meant to the men and women who heard it from Jesus's living, breathing mouth at that time? As Sayers wrote, "They had misunderstood practically everything Christ had ever said to them, but no matter; the thing made sense at last and the meaning was far beyond anything they had dreamed."[6]

Still, given the context of life in the first century, the sending out of this new body of Jesus Christ was bound to create new enemies. As long as they were on this earth, they could be sure of two things: God was with them, and they would encounter conflict.

Commissioned into Conflict

Even as soon as Pentecost, the disciples and their fellow believers caused a stir. When the Holy Spirit filled this small group of friends, many outsiders thought they were out of their minds, or drunk, or both. The transformation that took place as they gathered together drew such attention that people could not ignore them. It baffled the skeptics, angered the authorities, and attracted the seekers. This same promise of God's new creation spilled over into the disciples' lives and into bold new actions as well as bold new preaching.

What became the center of their proclamations each time Peter and the others stood before a crowd from that day forward? The good news that Christ's death and resurrection—which they had seen with their own eyes—offered the forgiveness of sins and life everlasting. As one commentator put it, "Peter speaks of the resurrection of Jesus from the dead as the basis of the believer's faith and hope and forgiveness. . . . It is not something for which Peter has to contend but rather is given as a basis for godly confidence."[7]

Yet the more he and the others spoke in this godly confidence, the more they encountered conflict and antagonism.

Everywhere they went, following the risen Lord meant counting the cost and paying a price. It meant making decisions that changed—and endangered—their lives even more. What would that have been like for this early group of middle-class converted Jews? Would they have to forsake all they knew? Would they be thrown into jail? Would they have to leave their homeland and everything they'd been familiar with—again? Would it require them to gather regularly for meals and prayer, worship and Scripture readings, just to maintain their courage? And how would they make ends meet? Would they have to pool their resources so they could continue in their mission to tell others about Jesus? What would it mean for their traditions as Jews to encounter non-Jews with this gospel truth?

We know from the book of Acts (and history certainly confirms it) that all of these questions confronted this little group, mostly because they took Christ's call and mission seriously. They'd been personally and corporately changed by the love with which Jesus pursued them—and now sent them. They took it so seriously that they inevitably confronted the political and religious leaders in the region each time they delivered the news of his kingdom. And since the risen Lord had also appeared to *five hundred* other men and women (see 1 Cor. 15:6), they too were given the same purpose: to wait for the Holy Spirit and then go into all the world, to take up their crosses as they followed the once dead, now alive God-man. From Mary, the women, and Cleopas and his companion to Peter, Thomas, John, and the others, each encountered the Living Christ, and they were changed; in response, they endured opposition whenever they told others of his life, and yet so many people believed their message that the world was never the same again.

It was the greatest word-of-mouth promotional campaign ever held. It still is.

But it did not come without great struggle. Many religious leaders, zealous rabbis, and civic authorities had no patience for this new radical group and saw them—and their message—as a rebellious disruption to the traditions of the land. As N. T. Wright said, "The world cannot cope with a Jesus who comes out of the tomb, who inaugurates God's new creation right in the middle of the old one."[8]

One of the church's greatest enemies, one who could not cope with this Jesus, was named Saul. Peter and Thomas were timid in comparison; Saul grew so angry at their words about the Messiah and the revolution Christ had incited that he felt morally justified to organize and implement a horrific persecution against the early church, one similar (in terror) to that of Hitler's Third Reich.

Consider these words of Luke's in Acts 8:1–4 (emphasis added) just after the disciple Stephen was stoned to death for claiming he knew and saw the risen Jesus:

And Saul was there, giving approval to his death. On that day a great persecution broke out against the church at Jerusalem, and all except the apostles were scattered throughout Judea and Samaria. Godly men buried Stephen and mourned deeply for him. *But Saul began to destroy the church. Going from house to house, he dragged off men and women and put them in prison.* Those who had been scattered preached the word wherever they went.

emphasis mine

If Peter or John or the others had any question of the danger their faith in the Lord Jesus would bring, it was confirmed with the vicious persecution from men like Saul. A Pharisee who trained under some of the most prominent rabbis in the land, Saul was determined to obliterate this new sect of Jesus-followers. He had received a traditional Jewish education and would have been conversant with Jewish traditions for interpreting the Scriptures and indeed the Prophets themselves. Nothing about Jesus or this new sect fit into his theology. If anything, to him these "Christ-followers" were heretics, criminals for breaking the law of God as Saul knew it. And their stubborn persistence in talking about the cruci-fied Jesus *as if he were now alive* only fueled his ire.

Obviously, Saul was not the only enemy of that early fel-lowship or of subsequent Christians since. The obedience Peter, John, and the others showed in waiting as Jesus had instructed them and then going when and where the Holy Spirit directed them became the impetus behind this new faith movement. Many others believed because of these leaders' journeys and yet, in so doing, also were threatened with their lives. In later years, numerous Christians—or "Little Christs," as Martin Luther defined them—were also crucified, burned at the stake, hung, or quartered. Many were thrown into captivity as slaves. Others were beheaded, exiled, or sent to jail. They were separated from their families and dragged from their homes to be put in prison. Some still are.

Being a Christian was no intellectual exercise or moral training for the early church. It cost all they had. It required a response that matched the sacrifice of their Lord, which only deepened the zeal of leaders like Saul who had been determined to prove them wrong by killing their movement. But there was one thing Saul hadn't yet realized: it wasn't flesh and blood he was fighting.

So in one of the most extraordinary true stories in ancient literature, the same risen Lord who'd appeared to these oth-ers decided also to love a brutal, angry murderer known as Saul. In Acts 9, Saul was on his way to the high priest "still breathing out murderous threats against the Lord's disciples" (v. 1). He was hoping the priest would provide the documents he'd need to give "to the synagogues in Damascus, so that if he found any there who belonged to the Way, whether men or women, he might take them as prisoners to Jerusalem" (v. 2). But as he neared Damascus on his journey, the cruel and violent Pharisee got the shock of his life: a fantastic light from heaven suddenly flashed around him, sending Saul to the ground. Then he heard a voice say to him, "Saul, Saul, why do you persecute me?" (v. 4).

I can imagine Saul shaking in the dirt, terrified at the visitation of such holiness given who he was and what he'd been doing. The words were probably barely audible from Saul's lips: "Who are you, Lord?" (v. 5).

" 'I am Jesus, whom you are persecuting,' he replied. 'Now get up and go into the city, and you will be told what you must do.' The men traveling with Saul stood there speechless; they heard the sound but did not see anyone. Saul got up from the ground, but when he opened his eyes he could see nothing. So they led him by the hand into Damascus. For three days he was blind, and did not eat or drink anything" (vv. 7–9).

Blinded by the living Word, leveled to the ground, and led like a desperate child to Damascus, Saul was the most unlikely convert of all. But why did Jesus ask Saul why he was persecuting *him*? After all, Christ was no longer walking the earth in human form, and Saul hadn't been present at the crucifixion to flog Christ or endorse his death. So what was Jesus talking about? How had Saul persecuted *him*?

It was this new body of Christ Saul had abused. As Jesus said in Matthew 25, "Whatever you do to the least of these, you do to me" (see v. 40). And so, because of the faithful testimonies of those early Christians, those willing to proclaim the truth of the gospel in spite of the consequences from men like Saul, the Lord was defending his own body, his beloved hands and feet and eyes, when he confronted Saul. Yet in the process and also because of their faithfulness, God was able to accomplish his purposes and confirm—again—his character of grace. In Saul's famous encounter with the risen Jesus on the Damascus road, we see how a once murderous, sinful, and evil man could be transformed into one of the Christian church's greatest communicators. From that time forward he was known as Paul.

To say that Paul's life was changed from that encounter would be an obvious understatement. It was upended, overturned, rearranged, and absolutely altered forever. So were the lives of those around him, as well as the early believers who—understandably—were a little afraid to join Paul in fellowship. Nonetheless, Paul's confrontation with the resurrected Jesus became the primary motivation behind his new life and ministry, as it had with this radical group of believers he had once sought to destroy. Paul's sermons in various cities (recorded in Acts) and his letters to the churches throughout the world encouraged, challenged, and formed the basis not just of a new theology but of an entirely new life. If Jesus was "really real" to anyone, it was Paul.

For him, the resurrection was the foundation on which all other decisions were made and on which any confidence could be built. It became the shield by which he, and all other Christians, could endure anything. It had to be; because of his newfound faith and proclamation of it, Paul himself went on to endure great opposition, persecution, tragedy, imprisonment, and affliction. The rest of the book of Acts and Paul's many letters to the churches also detail such suffering, violence, and hardship.

To Paul, the resurrection of Jesus was no clever idea, no mere afterthought to a belief system. It was everything. In fact, he referred to it fifty-three times in his writings throughout the New Testament. Why? Because, as he wrote in 1 Corinthians 15:17, "if Christ has not been raised, your faith is futile; you are still in your sins." It was a reality with more power than all the pagan legends and Jewish laws combined, the very fulfillment of all he'd ever hoped for or known from his own history. Yes, it was moving and compelling and dramatic, but it was no mere story to Paul. It knocked him flat. It changed him. His life was instantly disrupted, full of conflict, tension, and of course hope.

But because he too responded to Christ's love, we became the beneficiaries of some of the greatest theological works in Scripture. His letters were a means of discipleship, reminding all who read them of the power of the living God and that the resurrected Christ, in whom we live and move and have our being, is the Good News with which we're now entrusted.

Paul knew firsthand that this was not a nice plan or a moral formula or a value system but a living, breathing person who is with us always.

Yet from Christ's living presence, Paul also understood that as he—like us—introduced others to Jesus, some would believe. Some wouldn't. Some would be intrigued, and others would be antagonistic. Still, he warned, if just for this life Christ was their hope, they were to be pitied more than all. He was desperate for them to know the truth that had slapped him silly, the truth that Christ's risen life changed everything about them, every day and forever. No wonder he wrote to the Philippians in 3:10–11: "I want to know Christ and the power of his resurrection and the fellowship of sharing in his sufferings, becoming like him in his death, and so, somehow, to attain to the resurrection of the dead."

And no wonder he broadcast such news throughout the land.

Lessons on the Run

What enabled Paul to write such letters? Or Peter, Thomas, Mary, and the others to keep going in the midst of so much persecution and struggle? What made it possible for them to persevere in their faith not just with mild compliance but with *great joy*? In crowds, they exclaimed the news of Jesus as if their lives depended on it. In prison, they rejoiced that they were considered worthy of the suffering. In every journey and adventure, every gathering and tragedy, they did not merely complete a task; they lived a life that was overflowing with peace and grace. How could they?

Maybe the better question is, how could they *not*? After all, the God of creation had personally pursued each of them, inviting them to spend three years of their lives with him in human form and to put their trust in his promises. When he went to the cross, they reached an all-time low in their earthly existence. Their despair and grief overwhelmed them—until they got a glimpse of understanding about what had happened. And when he spent forty days *after his murder* with them—alive again—they knew beyond a doubt that Christ was who he said he was. His Holy Spirit confirmed it by dwelling in their spirits, and they became new men and women; they became Christ's new body.

They knew they'd been commissioned—like Jesus—to go into a world fraught with danger and hopelessness. They knew their lives were going to be threatened and that death was imminent, especially the more they talked about Christ. But they also knew that they—like the Lord—would rise again. Their hope was in the love of the living God, and the promise of eternity with him made every incident on earth pale in comparison.

In other words, the resurrection of Jesus Christ after his crucifixion formed the basis not only of their new faith but also of their perspectives about everything they encountered on earth. The more they focused on the risen Jesus, the more they could face whatever hardship or challenge came their way with courage and grace. They knew there was far more to this earthly life than what they saw and experienced in the day-to-day. Every part of their identities had been transformed by his "really real" presence, and that changed every agenda and attitude they had. Eugene Peterson put it this way: "Jesus' followers live resurrection-formed lives, not by watching him or imitating him or being influenced by him, but by being raised with him. It's formation-by-resurrection. It's the life itself—the God-breathed, Jesus-breathed beginning of who we are and who we become by the Holy Spirit, the Holy Breathing."[9]

Before his death, Jesus introduced himself to them through his deeds and words, the stories of which we can now read in the Gospel accounts. But he also formed his character in them through his Spirit; by breathing on them—filling up their lungs, beating in their hearts—he accomplished his deeds and words, just as he wants to do with us today. His holy breathing *on* them re-created them, raising them anew, sharing his resurrection life with them—with us—for the here and now.

The great news, then, about these forty days of Christ's time on earth after his death and his ensuing presence in the lives of the fellow believers we meet in the book of Acts, is that we, too, as modern people, can meet the man who likewise calls us to wait *so that* he can send us out. We too can receive the eternal perspective that motivated the early church *so that* we can endure any trial with an equal sense of joy and trust. We are the ones about whom Christ told Thomas, "Blessed are those who have not seen and yet have believed" (John 21:29). Though we might not be literal eyewitnesses, we are witnesses to the body of Christ throughout history and that continues to grow today. We see the physical-ness of Jesus in each other every time we walk out the door and especially every time we gather with fellow believers around prayer, Scripture, and worship. He lives indeed among us. We are formed together by his resurrection.

This is a reality we can be sure of, one more real than what we might see in the grittiness of daily life on earth. Christ, after all, never spiritualized his resurrection; in fact, during his forty-day journey he didn't walk into a single synagogue (that we know of), nor did he visit a spiritual revival or a Christian retreat. He did, however, drop by a couple of houses, stroll on a beach, share a few meals, and appear in a cemetery, on a few roads, and in an apartment.

In short, the risen Lord appeared in the ordinariness of life to this ordinary group of friends as an ordinary man. As Dr. Timothy Keller, pastor of Redeemer Presbyterian Church in New York City, distinguished in a recent sermon, Greek and Roman thinking at the time of Christ would have assumed a resurrected being—if there even was such a thing—to be only spirit. But Jesus appeared to his disciples in physical form, enjoying his human senses and admonishing his followers to do the same. If it were fiction, it wouldn't work. Likewise, Jewish thinking at the time would have expected a resurrected Messiah to be stately and regal and formidable—as they'd always hoped their king would be. But when Jesus appeared alive again, he did so as an ordinary man in ordinary places, his scars still evident and his body still needing food and walks and warmth.

Because he was both physical and ordinary and yet God incarnate, Christ provided for his followers—and for us—as Keller said, "a glimpse of our own futures. Christ's body risen and redeemed meant that was what our lives would be like in the future. In Jesus, we're looking at our own First Fruits from the dead."[10]

In Jesus, in the Spirit, in God the Father, and in his body of believers, we have both a future and a present community that is real now and full of joy for all times. That future, which of course has already begun, is what sustains us and inspires us to be his hands and his voice to a world in need of both.

Yet we cannot do it alone. Just as none in the early church was sent alone, so are we together privileged to carry the words of the Resurrected Lord as one body, in one mission, to those who need to hear the story anew. As we do, we will inevitably face challenge and opposition both from within the church and from the culture. Christ's reconciling work, however, keeps us moving forward.

The Point: Conversion

And so we come to the end of these narratives, knowing they have served as both a starting point and a blueprint for all who acknowledge Jesus as Lord of their lives. Of course, some would say that many, many people have been collectively deceived, sold a monumental lie about this historic figure, one that sent them to their own excruciating tragedies and deaths. Others look at the stories and can't help but claim that these Gospel accounts revealing the risen Jesus are in fact true and worth considering, containing a message of hope they simply cannot—and did not—keep to themselves.

Paul, Peter, Cleopas, Mary, and all the others we've met in these pages believed the proof of Jesus Christ. They felt wooed by and called to him and then sent by him with a unique purpose, specifically designed to accomplish the things God put them on the planet to do in the time they had. Some wrote. Some preached. Others served. Their lives suggest that this same God then offers the same to each of us today, *if* we too will consider the evidence of his life on earth as the impetus for all we do. The truth of Jesus Christ defines who we are.

But like these who have gone before us, we can be sure this new life will not be easy. We also will have to die daily *so that* we can be raised to new life with and through Christ's Spirit. Yet, in the strangest of paradoxes, the testimonies of the ages suggest that we can be raised with Jesus not someday, not in some far-off time zone that has no relevance for us in the work and lives we enjoy on earth. No, we're raised with him *now*. The pressure has been taken off; like the lives of Christ's followers testify, we cannot earn it or try harder for this gift of eternal life. It's already been secured for us.

Those first Christians were changed not by being more religious or by working at their spiritual lives. They were changed *only* when they encountered the person of resurrection, the life everlasting, "the radiance of God's glory" (Heb. 1:3). New life for them—and for us—begins *now*, at recognizing his sacrifice on the cross and in breathing in his resurrected life in every situation, knowing he will sustain us. It has been done, and is being completed in us, by the Word made flesh—if we believe.

In his commentary on Acts, N. T. Wright explained it beautifully:

> Part of the point about Jesus' resurrection is that it was the beginning of precisely that astonishing and world-shattering renewal. It wasn't just that he happened to be alive again, as though by some quirk of previously unsuspected "nature" or by some extraordinary "miracle" in which God did the impossible just to show how powerful he was, death suddenly

worked backwards in his particular case. It was, rather, that because on the cross, he had indeed dealt with the main force of evil, decay and death itself, the creative power of God, no longer thwarted as it had been by human rebellion, could at last burst forth and produce the beginning, the pilot project, of that joined-up heaven-and-earth reality which is God's plan for the whole world.[11]

Yes, the light burst through the darkness. The grief was turned to hope. The creative power of God transformed even the most sinful and desperate of men and women. And in so doing it brought forth life from death, abundance from nothing, and joy from sorrow. A tomb became a new garden, a beach fire became a movement, and a war became a backdrop for a story that transcended every culture and era, one that resonates throughout history with the question that comes to us still: what indeed would our lives—and our world—look like if we heard and believed the living voice of the man who was born to be King?

— IN-BETWEEN REFLECTION —

1. Why do you think Dorothy L. Sayers's radio plays had the impact they did? What kind of communication of the message of Christ's resurrection could be helpful today? How could God use your talents in similar ways?
2. The early church experienced great opposition to their faith. Have you experienced, or do you know of, similar opposition or persecution because of faith in Christ? What was it like? How did you, or others, get through?
3. What about Paul's life and story captures your imagination in a new way?
4. What does the ordinariness of the risen Jesus and the ordinariness of his body mean for you? How does it speak to you in your "ordinary" life and faith journey?

5. In what ways are you being called to wait so that you can be sent? In what ways can your community wait so that it can be sent to serve others with the love that abides forever?

PRAYER:

Light of the World, Light of Life, shine through us so that others might leave their darkness and come into your presence for all eternity. In Christ alone who is our hope, amen.

If there is no resurrection of the dead, then not even Christ has been raised. And if Christ has not been raised, our preaching is useless and so is your faith. More than that, we are then found to be false witnesses about God, for we have testified about God that he raised Christ from the dead. . . .

But Christ has indeed been raised from the dead, the firstfruits of those who have fallen asleep. For since death came through a man, the resurrection of the dead comes also through a man. For as in Adam all die, so in Christ all will be made alive. But each in his own turn: Christ, the firstfruits; then, when he comes, those who belong to him.

Paul, 1 Corinthians 15:13–15, 20–23

Notes

Chapter 1 Desperate Truth

1. T. R. Glover, *The Jesus of History* (New York: Association Press, 1920), 178.

2. J. R. R. Tolkien, quoted in Leland Ryken's *The Christian Imagination* (Colorado Springs: Shaw, 2002).

3. N. T. Wright, *The Resurrection of the Son of God* (Minneapolis: Augsburg Fortress Press, 2003), 570.

Chapter 2 Unlikely Witnesses

1. Arthur Stace quote, National Museum of Australia Canberra. "Stories from the Emotional Heart of Australia." www.nma.gov.au/exhibitions/now_showing/eternity/stories_from_the_emotional_heart_of_australia/.

2. Ignatius Jones quote, National Museum of Australia Canberra. "Stories from the Emotional Heart of Australia." www.nma.gov.au/exhibitions/now_showing/eternity/stories_from_the_emotional_heart_of_australia/.

3. Wright, *The Resurrection of the Son of God*, 34–35.

Chapter 3 Name's Sake

1. Hugh T. Kerr and John Mulder, *Conversions: The Christian Experience* (Grand Rapids: Eerdmans, 1983), 115–16.

2. Ibid.

3. Joyce Hollyday, "Sojourner Truth: A Pillar of Fire." *Sojourners*, December 1986.

4. Harriet Beecher Stowe quoted in the forward to Sojourner Truth's autobiography, *Narrative of Sojourner Truth*, 1850.

5. Sojourner Truth, quoted in Joyce Hollyday, "Sojourner Truth: A Pillar of Fire." *Sojourners*, December 1986.

6. Alice Mathews, *A Woman God Can Lead* (Grand Rapids: Discovery House, 1998), 330.

7. Eugene Peterson, *Living the Resurrection: The Risen Christ in Everyday Life* (Colorado Springs: NavPress, 2006), 26.

8. Mathews, *A Woman God Can Lead*, 330.

9. Sojourner Truth, *Narrative of Sojourner Truth*.

10. Frederick Buechner, *The Faces of Jesus: A Life Story* (Brewster, MA: Paraclete Press, 2004), 87.

Chapter 4 Teachable Moments

1. Peterson, *Living the Resurrection*, 61.

2. Ibid., 62

3. Buechner, *Faces of Jesus*, 88.

Chapter 5 Sensory Appeal

1. Isabella Stewart Gardner on the creation of her museum, 1917, http://www.gardnermuseum.org/collection/overview.asp

2. Leslie Newbigin, *The Light Has Come: An Exposition of the Fourth Gospel* (Grand Rapids: Eerdmans, 1982), 270.

Chapter 6 Doubting Voices

1. C. S. Lewis, *The Lion, the Witch and the Wardrobe* (New York: HarperTrophy, Harper Collins Publishers, 1950), 46.

2. Ibid., 47.

3. Ibid., 48.

4. Buechner, *Faces of Jesus*, 8.

5. Wright, *The Resurrection of the Son of God*, 677.

6. Buechner, *Faces of Jesus*, 90.

Chapter 7 Beach Fires

1. Dorothy Day, *The Long Loneliness*, quoted in Robert Coles, *Dorothy Day: A Radical Devotion* (Reading, MA: Addison Wesley Publishing Company, 1987), 62.

2. Ibid., 52.

3. www.catholiceducation.org/articles/abortion/ab0063.html.

4. I have more thoroughly explored Peter's life and journey recorded in Scripture in my book *Reckless Faith: Living Passionately as Imperfect Christians* (Colorado Springs: Shaw Publishing, 2003).

5. Newbigin, *The Light Has Come*, 277.

6. Ibid., 278.

7. N. T. Wright, *Surprised by Hope: Rethinking Heaven, the Resurrection, and the Mission of the Church* (New York: HarperOne, 2008), 72–73.

Chapter 8 Sent Again

1. Dr. J. W. Welch, in the foreword of Dorothy L. Sayers's book of plays, *The Man Born to Be King: A Play-Cycle on the Life of Our Lord and Saviour Jesus Christ* (London: Victor Gollancz Ltd, 1969), 11. Presented by the British Broadcasting Corporation, Dec. 1941–Oct. 1942.

2. Ibid., 12.

3. Ibid., 9.

4. Ibid., 13.

5. Ibid., 16.

6. Dorothy L. Sayers, "The Triumph of Easter," in *Letters to a Diminished Church: Passionate Arguments for the Relevance of Christian Doctrine* (Nashville: Thomas Nelson, 2004), 124.

7. Paul Barnett, *Is the New Testament Reliable?* (Downers Grove, IL: InterVarsity, 2003), 114.

8. Wright, *Surprised by Hope*, 68.

9. Peterson, *Living the Resurrection*, 109.

10. Timothy J. Keller, "I Am Sending You" (sermon, Redeemer Presbyterian Church, New York, March 30, 2008).

11. N. T. Wright, *Acts for Everyone: Part One* (Louisville: Westminster John Knox Press, 2008).

Bibliography

Good writing always inspires me to want to write well, just as good preaching inspires good theology, which we hope, is lived out in the day to day. The following resources have helped me think—and I hope write—better about the anchor of our Christian faith, the living person of Jesus Christ who continues to inspire us with new and creative works. I offer them here for you as an ongoing muse as well.

Barnett, Paul. *Is the New Testament Reliable?* Downers Grove, IL: InterVarsity, 2003.

Bock, Darrell L. *Luke*. Vol. 3 of The IVP New Testament Commentary Series. Leicester, UK: Inter-Varsity Press, 1994.

Bible Gateway.com. *The International Bible Commentary with the New International Version*. Grand Rapids: Zondervan, 1999.

Buechner, Frederick. *The Faces of Jesus: A Life Story*. Brewster, MA: Paraclete Press, 2004.

Coles, Robert. *Dorothy Day: A Radical Devotion*. Reading, MA: Addison Wesley Publishing Company, 1987.

Day, Dorothy. *Selected Writings: By Little and by Little*. Edited by Robert Ellsberg. Maryknoll, NY: Orbis Books, 1992.

Grant, Michael. *Saint Peter: A Biography*. New York: Barnes and Noble Books, 1994.

Hollyday, Joyce. "Sojourner Truth: A Pillar of Fire." *Sojourners*, December 1986.

Holy Bible: The New International Version Study Bible. Grand Rapids: Zondervan, 1985.

Kadlecek, Jo. *Desperate Women of the Bible: Lessons on Passion from the Gospels*. Grand Rapids: Baker, 2006.

———. *Reckless Faith: Living Passionately as Imperfect Christians, 8 Studies from the Life of Peter*. Colorado Springs: Shaw Publishing, 2003.

Keller, Timothy J. "I Am Sending You." Sermon, Redeemer Presbyterian Church, New York, March 30, 2008.

———. *The Prodigal God: Recovering the Heart of the Christian Faith*. New York: Penguin, 2008.

Kerr, Hugh T., and John Mulder. *Conversions: The Christian Experience*. Grand Rapids: Eerdmans, 1983.

Lewis, C. S. *The Lion, the Witch and the Wardrobe*. New York: HarperTrophy, Harper Collins Publishers, 1950.

Mathews, Alice. *A Woman God Can Lead*. Grand Rapids: Discovery House, 1998.

National Museum of Australia Canberra. "Stories from the Emotional Heart of Australia." www.nma.gov.au/exhibitions/now_showing/eternity/stories_from_the_emotional_heart_of_australia/.

Newbigin, Leslie. *The Light Has Come: An Exposition of the Fourth Gospel*. Grand Rapids: Eerdmans, 1982.

PBS Frontline. *From Jesus to Christ: The First Christians*. Documentary series, April 1998, www.pbs.org/wgbh/pages/frontline/shows/religion/.

Peterson, Eugene. *Living the Resurrection: The Risen Christ in Everyday Life*. Colorado Springs: NavPress, 2006.

Russ, Dan. *Flesh and Blood Jesus: Learning to Be Fully Human from the Son of Man*. Grand Rapids: Baker, 2008.

Sayers, Dorothy L. *The Man Born to Be King: A Play-Cycle on the Life of Our Lord and Saviour Jesus Christ. Presented by* the British Broadcasting Corporation, Dec. 1941–Oct. 1942. London: Victor Gollancz Ltd., 1969.

———. "The Triumph of Easter." In *Letters to a Diminished Church: Passionate Arguments for the Relevance of Christian Doctrine*. Nashville: Thomas Nelson, 2004.

Strobel, Lee. *The Case for Easter: A Journalist Investigates the Evidence for the Resurrection*. Grand Rapids: Zondervan, 1998.

Truth, Sojourner, and Olive Gilbert. 1850. *Narrative of Sojourner Truth, a Northern Slave, Emancipated from Bodily Servitude by the State of New York, in 1828*. Documenting the American South. University Library, The University of North Carolina at Chapel Hill, 2000. http://docsouth.unc.edu/neh/truth50/truth50 .html.

Wright, N. T. *Acts for Everyone: Part One*. Louisville: Westminster John Knox Press, 2008.

———. *The Resurrection of the Son of God*. Minneapolis: Augsburg Fortress Press, 2003.

———. *Surprised by Hope: Rethinking Heaven, the Resurrection, and the Mission of the Church*. New York: HarperOne, 2008.

Acknowledgments

New life is tricky. The idea of resurrection is as problematic to high-tech modern minds as it was to those in the first century. And yet it is this very impossibility that remains the center of our Christian faith, the compass from which many navigate their contemporary lives and the power that still changes hard hearts and sick souls.

Jesus does indeed live.

I know this to be true because of the many gifted, smart, and devoted women and men I've met since I began studying the stories that became the material for these chapters. Their lives testify to his. And their friendships—new and old—helped me think through the implications of these enormously profound narratives so that we all might reflect the delight and hope of the resurrection of Jesus Christ. At retreats or conferences, over coffee or wine, in offices or living rooms, their discussions, questions, and admirably informed faith helped me see things I hadn't—or couldn't—on my own.

I'm grateful, then, to these friends and their local churches who invited me to share and explore together the Good News of the Risen Lord: Cheryl Baird and Blanchard Alliance

Church in Wheaton, IL; Debbie Lloyd Jobe, Kathy Hudson and Willow Bend Church in Plano, TX; Debbie Haliday and the Rest and Renewal Women's Retreat in Ojai, CA; Brenda Walker and Church in the City in Denver, CO; Heather Kinder, Christine Metzger and Redeemer Hoboken Church in Hoboken, NJ; Margot Eyring, Pastor Del Glick and Washington Community Fellowship in Washington, D.C.; Carol Slager and Modesto Christian Reformed Church in Modesto, CA. Thank you for the privilege and fun of being a part of your communities during your weekend retreats; your faith and presence in my life has contributed much to this book.

I'm also particularly thankful for specific individuals who traveled through these great stories with me: my agent Lee Hough, who is exactly what every author hopes for in an agent, a wise advocate and friend; Bob Hosack, my editor at Baker, whose ongoing support of my work is humbling and deeply appreciated; artists Norm and Jean Jones, whose weekly presence in our home Bible study group has been delightfully instructive; Elisabeth Coen, Eileen Sommi, and Pamela Brown Peterside, fellow writers whose love for and trust in the resurrected Jesus inspires me; my colleagues/friends Laurie Truschel and Casey Cooper at Gordon College, whose early morning commitments to study these stories with me and wonderfully awake insights were a profound gift; and of course, Chris Gilbert, my husband, whose contributions to this book are so great his name probably should be on it well.

To those writers, theologians, and pastors whose works I've learned from, to those friends whose support I've leaned on, and to those students and colleagues at Gordon College whose prayers and patience I've depended on while writing this, thank you. You are indeed proof that Jesus Christ is no longer dead.

And finally, to you, Reading Friend, thank you for choosing to read this book, hold it in your hands, turn its pages with your fingers, even when the demands on your life are no doubt great and real. I pray it has been a valuable journey, one which will continue to move you closer to the Living Word so that others, too, might encounter the One who conquered death that we might know life.

May you always have daffodils.

Jo Kadlecek is a former waitress, soccer player, and debate coach who has always been hooked on a good story. Because of her love for stories, she has taught writing and literature classes at several colleges and conferences, is a frequent teacher at church retreats, and has written over thirteen books, including four novels. She holds masters' degrees in humanities and communication. Currently, she is the senior writer at Gordon College in Wenham, MA, a top Christian liberal arts college just north of Boston, where she also serves on the faculty, teaching journalism classes. She and her husband, Chris—a filmmaker from Australia—love the ocean, history, and cities, and are leaders in their local church. For more information on Jo's books and stories, please visit, www.lamppostmedia. net. To read her blog on journalism, visit http://JoReporter .blogspot.com, or to find out more about Gordon College, visit www.gordon.edu.